WORKING TOWARDS PARTNERSHIP IN THE EARLY YEARS

Gillian Pugh
(Head, Under Fives Unit, National Children's Bureau)
and
Erica De'Ath
(Chief Executive, Foundation for the Study of Infant Deaths)

NATIONAL CHILDREN'S BUREAU

Working towards Partnership in
the Early Years

© National Children's Bureau, 1989

ISBN 0 902 81742 6

Published by National Children's Bureau
8 Wakley Street
London EC1V 7QE
Telephone 01-278 9441

Printed and bound in Great Britain by
Biddles Ltd, Guildford and King's Lynn

Contents

By the same authors

The Needs of Parents: practice and policy in parent education. Macmillan. 1984

Working with parents: a training resource pack. National Children's Bureau. 1986.

Partnership in Action, volumes 1 and 2 (with Geoff Aplin and Margaret Moxon). National Children's Bureau. 1987.

Self help and Family Centres. Erica De'Ath, National Children's Bureau. 1985

Services for under fives. Developing a co-ordinated approach. Gillian Pugh, National Children's Bureau. 1988

1. Introduction

Parent involvement, family support, participation, consumer involvement and partnership between parents and professionals have become fashionable concepts in recent years. The rights, roles and responsibilities of both parents and professionals have been the subject of frequent debate, and few of those who work with children in the health, education and social welfare fields can be unaware of the new dimensions that this brings to their work. But what do these various terms mean? Does partnership really exist or is it simply empty rhetoric? And for whom are the supposed benefits intended? Is it intended to enhance children's development? Or to change parents' behaviour in some way? Or to build up their confidence in their own roles as parents and educators? Or is it for the benefit of professionals, and if so will it increase their understanding of children's home backgrounds, or merely provide them with an extra pair of hands on a busy day?

In the course of a national survey of parent education and support, published as *The Needs of Parents: Practice and Policy in Parent Education* (Pugh and De'Ath 1984) it became apparent that several factors had a bearing both on how parents viewed their own role as parents and on how they saw their relationships with the increasing number of professional child care experts with whom they came in touch during the early years of their children's lives. Parents felt under increasing pressure to live up to society's ideal of perfect parenthood and to provide for their child's physical, intellectual and emotional development. Yet as the media promoted such images of family life and parental responsibilities, many found themselves in the isolation of their homes, anxious and guilty, unsure of which way to turn as they experienced conflicting advice from books, television and child care experts.

The conflicting messages of parents as 'deficient' or as 'expert' also became clear in this study. The availability of support for *all* families was clearly lacking: parents were often seen as falling into one of two camps. Either they were coping adequately and were felt to need no assistance at all, or they fell below an accepted level of providing 'good enough parenting' and became the focus of immediate state intervention. In addition, some of the 'adequate' and competent parents often felt their role diminished and their self-confidence undermined by the way they were treated by professionals. However, in those schemes and centres where professionals and parents 'worked with' parents rather than 'did things to' them, it was clear that effective relationships between professionals and parents could be created if built on notions of partnership and mutual respect.

In working in new ways with parents, developing roles as enablers and catalysts as well as teachers or fixers of problems, professionals were, however, also finding that their own values, attitudes and feelings were often at odds with those of the parents. The question of different values was also at the root of the dilemma perceived in many parent education programmes, a dilemma which reflected the different ideological and political bases from which such programmes had been established. In essence, whose values were these programmes to reflect? Were they to be seen as a means of social control whereby parents (and working class parents in particular) were taught how to be 'better' parents, and how to interact properly with their children; or were they to be a means to social change and personal growth, whereby parents – and mothers in particular – were given encouragement and self-confidence to take greater control of their lives, and, where necessary, to challenge the system – and the professionals within the system?

Another issue was the role that parents themselves were beginning to play in schools and pre-school centres. The notion of parent involvement was still largely seen by centres – and by some parents – as being on the terms laid down by the centre – you come and help us in the ways that we think fit. But the parent education study pointed to large numbers of parents in playgroups, family groups, home-visiting schemes and so on who, given adequate preparation and support, were well able to lead groups, visit homes and offer support to other parents themselves.

2. The Partnership Project

This report draws on the results of a three year study set up following the work on parent education to explore the notion of partnership between parents and professionals in pre-school services. It differed from previous studies of parent involvement in being specifically concerned with the concept of partnership, and in being multi-disciplinary in focus, rather than working only in schools. The project was funded by the Department of Health and Social Security from 1983–1986, with a small additional grant from the Scottish Office. Members of the project team were Gillian Pugh (who directed the project) and Erica De'Ath and two part-time colleagues – Geoff Aplin from the Department of Social Administration and Social Work at Glasgow University, and Margaret Moxon, a teacher from Newcastle. Martin Bradley, at the time at Liverpool Institute of Higher Education, worked part-time with the project from 1983–4. The aims of the project were:

- to explore the extent to which services for families with children under five are planned, implemented and delivered in partnership with those families for whom they are intended;

- to identify and examine a number of initiatives in which a working partnership is achieved between parents and workers in the health, education, social services and voluntary sectors;

- to disseminate information and promote discussion of parent-professional partnership.

As the project progressed, so little was identified that could truly be described as partnership that it was decided to extend the brief to encompass the whole area of 'parent involvement', and answers were sought to such questions as:

What is it about services and schemes which help and hinder a close working relationship between parents and professionals?

What reasons do professionals give for wanting to work with parents?

What is partnership, and how does it differ from support, involvement and participation?

Do parents want to be more involved in planning, running and managing pre-school services?

What roles can and do parents play in pre-school services?

What new skills are required by both parents and professionals as they take on new roles?

Who makes the decisions about parent involvement, where does the power lie, and whose values does the relationship reflect?

What are some of the benefits and disadvantages of partnership with parents?

In working in the education, health, social services and voluntary sectors, we sought out centres, groups, schemes and nurseries in which real attempts were being made to achieve a working partnership between professionals and parents. Members of the project team visited some 130 centres (the term 'centre' is used to include all types of provision – nursery schools and classes, day nurseries, playgroups, family centres etc.) in all, and chose 16 for further study. Accounts of twelve of these are published in two volumes of *Partnership in Action; working with parents in pre-school centres* (Pugh *et al* 1987 a & b). Other publications from the project include the edited papers from nine conferences – *Partnership Papers* (De'Ath and Pugh 1985–6, Aplin and Tristram 1987), and a training resource pack for professionals wishing to examine their values and attitudes and increase their skills in working with parents, entitled *Working with Parents* (De'Ath and Pugh 1986).

3. The Case for Parent Involvement

The discussion of parent involvement and the arguments advanced for reassessing the relationship between parents and professionals have tended to vary in focus and in emphasis, reflecting the different ideological and philosophical bases of pre-school services. Some arguments focus on the educational gains made by children if parents are more involved in supporting their children's learning. Others are more concerned with parents' rights as consumers and rate-payers to participate in the services that they and their children use. A more recent argument has noted the benefits reaped by parents themselves in a closer involvement with the centre attended by their child, in terms of increased understanding and self-confidence (see Pugh and De'Ath 1984). The voluntary sector has shown how well able parents are to set up and run their own groups, and to take on roles as workers and providers of services. And in the health field there is a growing acknowledgement that as parents are their children's main health carers, then it is important that they are recognised and treated as such by health professionals (Mayall 1986).

Education

The notion of parent involvement, if not partnership, has been most thoroughly debated in the context of the education system, where two main themes can be identified: an awareness of the effect of social class and of parental aspirations on children's performance in school; and the rights of parents to be more closely involved in their children's education. Space does not permit a detailed examination of the social, psychological and political theories that govern the current debate, and they have in any case been well rehearsed elsewhere (for example, Smith 1980, Tizard *et al* 1981). Suffice it here to pick out one or two of the main issues as they relate to early childhood education.

In the early sixties, in response to a concern for the under-achievement of many working class children, researchers began to look at the effect that parents' attitudes might have on educational attainment. Research commissioned by the Plowden report (1967) confirmed earlier work of Douglas (1964, 1968) in concluding that 'the variation in parental attitudes can account for more of the variations in children's school achievement than either the variation in home circumstances or in schools'. The report's emphasis on encouraging parental participation in school, and the particular problems presented by working class children in this respect, have powerfully influenced teachers' attitudes towards parents in the last twenty years.

The Plowden report argued that 'one of the essentials for educational advance is a closer partnership between the two parties to every child's education', a partnership that it saw as needing to be 'more than just in name! To achieve this it recommended a programme of visits, open evenings and reports, but whilst these recommendations might ensure that parents were given more information, they hardly amounted to a partnership. They made no acknowledgement of what parents may have to offer the school for example, of teachers consulting with and listening to what parents have to say; or of sharing in management or decision-making. And although there is some recognition that the ideas and values of the school and community might be different, it is clear that the relationship is to be on the school's terms if education is to 'make up for the environment from which the children come'. Even the work of the Educational Priority Area projects that followed Plowden (Halsey, 1972) did not fully confront the divergent values of school and community, and as Tizard (1971) has pointed out, the issue of decision-making within the school, and the accountability of the teachers to parents and the community, was not raised.

The other major influence in the sixties was the work of psychologists such as Hunt (1961) and Bloom (1964) whose work on the nature and development of intelligence and early learning challenged earlier assumptions that intelligence was in some way fixed and predetermined. If in Bloom's words 'about fifty per cent of intellectual development takes place between conception and the age of five', and if intelligence could be modified, then, as the American Head Start programme was to try to prove, perhaps the cognitive performance of children in disadvantaged families could be improved by systematic structured curricula for such children. In reviewing these programmes in 1974, Bronfenbrenner made a number of points that were to influence pre-school programmes in Britain. In summary, he suggested that:-

- short sharp educational inoculations had little effect on the children or their families. A sustained continuous programme of support for families was felt to be more appropriate in order to achieve long-term gains from intervention.

- deficit models which attribute lower levels of cognitive performance, poor social skills and deviant behaviour to children from low income families, needed to be challenged. Expectations of teachers for children from such families were low. Parents had little confidence in their own ability to assist in their children's education.

- the influence on young children of their homes and their community environments were complex and powerful. Educational strategies could not be separated from the social contexts within which they operated.

- strategies which actively included parents in early childhood education seemed to be more effective in terms of long term gains than those which did not.

Although there is continuing evidence (see Clement *et al* 1984) of the long term gains of some of these programmes, the data is insufficiently detailed to indicate what types of curricula are most effective, or what 'active involvement' of parents actually means. However, in reviewing the implications of the American research for Britain, Woodhead (1985) points out that if the complex data is seen as a transactional model, then improved early performance, higher teacher expectation, increased pupil motivation and increased parental aspirations become mutually reinforcing. He concludes that pre-school intervention programmes are powerful in 'engineering, reinforcing and sustaining parental aspirations and interest in their children's education'.

Apart from the lone voice of Margaret McMillan in the first quarter of the century arguing that mothers had a right to participate in and manage the nursery schools their children attended, little was heard until the late 1970s of the rights of parents as consumers to a say in how schools should educate their children. The publication of the Taylor report on school management (DES 1977) and the Warnock report on special educational needs (DES 1978), and subsequent legislation in 1980 and 1981, together with the 1988 Education Act, ensure a greater involvement of parents in the management of schools and in their children's learning. But if parents are not given support in taking up appointment on governing bodies, and if there is no mechanism by which they can represent and account to the wider body of parents, these greater rights can be regarded as little more than tokens.

One of the difficulties in establishing partnership is the complexity of a system that has many partners – central government, local government, school governors, teachers and parents – and few clearly defined roles or lines of accountability. One way of clarifying roles and obligations would be to implement the recommendations of a report on home school liaison in Europe, which suggested that the shift should be away from rights and towards duties. Macbeth (1984) proposed a school and family concordat, whereby in return for a place at school, parents would sign a 'parents contract' undertaking to cooperate with the school in specific ways. The school in turn would also have liaison obligations to parents and 'with mutual commitments clearly understood from the start, parents and teachers would be able to develop a friendly professional partnership'.

Health Services

Consumer and community participation is also an issue in the health service, although it is not easy for parents to participate either individually or collectively in decisions about health and the health service. The aims of the World Health Organisation declaration drawn up at Alma Ata and proposing a world strategy for attaining positive health for all by the year 2000 includes the words 'The people have the right and duty to participate individually and collectively in the planning and implementation of their health care' (WHO 1978). The declaration suggests that the community should be involved in assessing the situation; in defining problems and setting priorities; in planning primary health care priorities; and in carrying out activities. 'This implies an acceptance by individuals of a high degree of responsibility for their own health care'. Although Britain was a signatory to the WHO declaration, the National Health Service has never been democratically managed, and individual and community participation in health services seem to have been particularly elusive. There is still no integration of community, hospital and general practitioner child health services and while a child health care working party of paediatricians and health visitors recommends explicit acknowledgement of the parents role as primary child health carer (Hall *et al* 1989), the proposals being put forward within the 1989 government review of the National Health Service appear to suggest less rather than more potential for parent and consumer involvement in the planning of services.

The arguments in support of partnership put a heavy responsibility on parents on behalf of their children. When the first health visitors started knocking on doors in the mid-nineteenth century they recognised that 'in the future the most important advance will come from an appreciation by the people themselves of the value of good health' (Robinson 1982). This view more recently informed the thinking of the Court committee (Committee on Child Health Services, 1976), whose philosophy can be summed up in their statement that 'we have found no better way to raise a child than to reinforce the ability of his parents to do so'. In reviewing the place of the child health services in supporting families in their health giving role, the report suggests that 'future improvements in the health and development of children depend as much upon the beliefs and behaviour of parents as on the services provided'. It talks about enabling parents to 'exercise their responsibility for their children' and urges professionals to encourage parents in this respect rather than usurping their responsibility:

'Professionals should see themselves as partners with parents; prepared and willing to give them explanation and advice about their children's health . . . The need is for a service that is geared to ensuring that parents are well informed and increasingly involved in their children's development and health, and which from the start will enable them to feel confident in their ability to care for their children' (op cit, 1976).

Recent research has shown that mothers do indeed see themselves as responsible for the promotion of their children's health, and have a good understanding of how they should go about trying to achieve the optimum health care (Mayall, 1986). Mothers cope with most episodes of illness without professional help and in this respect also they are their children's health carers. This study also showed, however, that the poor material circumstances of half the parents in the study – low income, bad housing conditions, and the stress of daily life – hampered their ability to put into practice what they knew to be appropriate.

One project which has worked specifically with parents in disadvantaged areas and has taken partnership as its central theme is the Child Development Programme, funded by the van Leer Foundation. Lowe (1986) describes the project as being a structured but very flexible form of health visiting which not only aims to achieve a more equal relationship between client and health visitor, but also engenders and encourages self-reliance and increased self-esteem and confidence on the part of the family. As the introductory booklet on the project puts it

'the project aims to persuade health visitors to modify the traditional approach, substituting a cooperative approach in which the visitor and parent jointly discuss strategies and work out as equals how best to help the child. For this, the visitor must openly recognise that the parent is the expert on her own child, while the visitor has an expertise in knowing about development in general, (Barker 1984).

Preliminary research results show increased take-up of immunisation, improvements in the quality of children's meals (and in parents' enjoyment in cooking them) and improvements in children's concentration and social behaviour (Lowe 1986). The project clearly has an important contribution to make to health visitor training and to how health professionals relate to the families they are working with. But in this respect in particular it brings us back to the dilemma faced by professionals in working with families whose value systems they do not share. Barker (1984) confronts this when he says

> 'The programme . . considers that if there are customs and ideas which promote the development of young children – even if these practices tend to be mainly those of the middle class – they should be made available to parents at all levels of social disadvantage or advantage; to deny parents access to such ideas is cultural elitism and may reinforce class, ethnic or other barriers'.

And although the project claims to be about partnership, the intervention health visitor quoted in the following passage from the report is clear about the terms on which the partnership is to be based: 'A big problem when we started this intervention as health visitors and saw the need for change in many families, was the hurdle that we had to get over in persuading the parents to recognise that there is a need for change, because they can't see it half the time'. The guidance offered to health visitors by the project team through training and support is very thorough, but as they admit, new ways of working present considerable problems to 'dominant health visitors who have difficulty in suppressing the urge to tell parents what to do'.

A final argument for the need for partnership between health professionals and parents is the changing pattern of childhood illness and disability. As Nicholl (1986) has argued, preventing, detecting and treating socio/psychological problems such as emotional and behaviour disorders, as well as physical disorders such as asthma and partial hearing loss, can only be done in close association with parents. The growing number of health districts in which parents are now given responsibility for keeping their own children's health records (Chaplais 1986 National Children's Bureau 1987) is one acknowledgement of the reality of this partnership.

Social Services

Nowhere has this challenge to change been more widely recognised in principle, if not in practice than in child welfare services. The Seebohm Report (1968) on the reorganisation of local authority personal social services urged the new social services departments to consider how clients might be more involved in decision-making and service delivery. The principle of client participation was argued on several grounds: that consumers interests were not identical to those of the service providers, that consumers have strong views about the appropriate level and standards of service, and that there needed to be a shift in the distribution of power between consumers and service providers. While government policy states that there should be a range of facilities available so that parents may choose what best meets their own and their children's needs, such a range is not available. If parents felt that they were entitled to child care services they might more readily challenge the workers and policy makers and argue for changes to provide a more appropriate range of services.

The Seebohm Report supported the community development approach stating that 'the community is both the provider as well as the recipients . . . . implicit in the idea of a community-orientated family service is a belief in the importance of the maximum participation of individuals and groups'. Unfortunately, many of the proposals were not implemented and the Barclay Report (1982) in advocating a community social work approach was in effect repeating many of the Seebohm recommendations.

There is an uneasy tension in looking at parent involvement with statutory social service provision, which derives from the two-fold presumption that parents are the primary carers of their children and have responsibility for them, and that some parents are less able to fulfil these responsibilities than others and the state needs to intervene to protect the child. This has resulted in situations where parents are not provided with help and support when they need it and ask for it, and other occasions when parents find that decisions are being made about their children without their involvement or agreement. Even in centres where trusting and open relationships have developed between staff and parents, the impact of suspected or actual sexual abuse on the developing partnership can be traumatic and long lasting (see for example Gilkes 1989).

It is government policy that public provision of childcare services should be concentrated on those with greatest need, that is, families with particular health or social needs. Many local authorities have changed their criteria and priorities for day nursery places, and educating and working with parents is seen as an important part of the work, rather than merely providing day care for children. This change of practice has also been reflected in the development of parent 'contracts' in some local authorities. Such contracts are designed to reach an agreed contractual arrangement with parents to establish the goals, objectives and activities for the family placement at the day nursery. As van der Eyken (1984) points out

> 'the development of 'family contracts' not only introduces a new element – parental responsibility – into day care, but it may also fundamentally affect the relationship between the service, staff and parents.'

While the general acceptance of parents in day nurseries and the growing development of parents' rooms, mother and toddler groups and social activities is welcome, the parent involvement on offer is still very much on the terms set down by the day nursery. Parents are encouraged to take part in practical tasks and in fund raising but there have been few attempts to involve them in the management of the day nursery, training activities, decision-making or use of resources.

Despite the general acceptance of parent involvement in day nurseries (many of which are now called family centres) there seems to have been little training for the workers. It is important that all those working in the day nursery understand the purpose of involving parents. Merely including a parent in an assessment session of the child's dexterity or cognition is not enough; parents need to be told why certain tasks are given or skills encouraged so that they can see beyond whether their child can or can't do it!

There is a fundamental dilemma for workers in trying to involve parents and encourage openness and trust when the child's safety must remain the priority. Although three quarters of day nursery placements in one study (van der Eyken, 1984) were found to be referrals from health visitors and social workers, many placements are voluntary and not in the context of legal proceedings. The ultimate aim of most local authority day nurseries and family centres is to enable parents to develop their potential as parents and take full responsibility for their child's care, safety and development. As Eyeington & Godfrey (1985) point out 'If this is to happen it is essential that the parents recover their sense of worth as parents'. The danger is that parents may feel that things are being done to them rather than see the possibility of working together, parents and professionals, to create and maintain a more satisfying family life. In the words of van der Eyken (1984)

> 'instead of seeing the day nursery as a service, to be used by parents, a

placement within a nursery may take on the role of an 'intervention strategy', in which both parents and children are actively involved, and whose outcome is to be monitored.'

The new guidelines for the protection of children from abuse now accept the general presumption of parental involvement. This is an important change arising from six cases taken to the European Court of Human Rights which cited failure to involve parents in decision-making as a factor in their judgements. The guidelines state:

'Parents need to know the reasons for professional concern, the statutory powers, duties and roles of agencies involved, their own legal rights and the changes in the family's situation which the agencies consider necessary or desirable in the interest of the child. Openness and honesty and the ability of professional staff to use authority appropriately are an essential basis on which to build a foundation of understanding between parents and professionals.' (DHSS, 1988, p. 29).

Equally, if parents are to be involved in review sessions this should be a genuine desire to review the situation from everyone's perspective and not an attempt to get parents to agree to what has already been decided at a pre-review meeting without the parents. As Blom Cooper has pointed out, it is pointless drawing up detailed action plans for the protection and development of a child unless everyone, including the parents caring for the child, is involved and committed to making that action plan work.

Voluntary and Private Sector Provision

Partnership between parents and workers in the voluntary non-profit making sector and the private sector is complicated by the diversity and scale of schemes and approaches. The limited extent of day care and nursery education in Britain has led to a proliferation of services run by non-statutory agencies, such that the range and number of places they offer is considerably greater than those available from local authorities. For example, playgroups now cater for nearly 60% of children of three and four. There is also a growing private sector provision such as contractual partnerships between parents and nannies, workplace nurseries, or independent nurseries or schools where the partnership is one of consumer/provider or a shared enterprise in the provision of child care.

The Wolfenden Report (1978) identified four different roles played by the voluntary sector – pioneer of services; provider of services complementary, additional or alternative to the statutory provision; sole provider of services; and, pressure group seeking change in policy and provision. The Barclay Report (1982) on social work described four main types of non-statutory providers of care – informal carers and neighbourhood networks; mutual aid groups (strangers with common particular difficulties); volunteers (individuals offering their services); and, formal voluntary organisations (with paid professional staff). In addition, there are the two largest providers of services to young children – the self-help approach of parent-run playgroups with their emphasis on personal growth through involvement and responsibility; and day care offered on a private basis by childminders on their own homes.

Many of the approaches within the non-statutory sector are founded on a presumption of parent involvement and responsibility and on concepts of partnership, but it is not always easy to disentangle who the partnership is between, nor indeed whether the workers see themselves as professionals or as parents or perhaps as both.

Seven main factors can be identified to explore the rapid development, context and extent of parent involvement and partnership within the non-statutory sector.

1. The changing use of day nurseries, such that the primary function is no longer provision of daycare, but rather a focus on children 'at risk' with a presumption of working with the parents to address emotional and social needs.

2. Provision by other parents, which has arisen through necessity. The growth in the use of childminders reflects not only the needs of working mothers for child care but also the greater acceptability of mother substitutes rather than group care for children. However, partnership between childminder and parent over the care of the child cannot be assumed.

3. Provision by groups of parents through the creation of playgroups, which acknowledge both the needs of young children for collective group experiences and of the mothers in sharing and contributing to the developmental needs of their child and other children through play.

4. A clear shift over the last 25 years from paternalistic philanthropy to community regeneration and self-determination. This has arisen both within traditional voluntary organisations, with a move away from baby adoption and day care to family centres and neighbourhood work, encouraging self-development and involvement of parents in decision-making processes; and in the growing numbers of women at home who were dissatisfied with

inappropriate or non-existing services and began to create and develop their own services (National Childbirth Trust, Gingerbread, PPA, NAWCH, etc).

5. An acknowledgement that parents do need informal support in their community. Research on Head Start (as noted above) has indicated that an educational programme in isolation has no real lasting benefit without continued support, and parents knew themselves there were times when they needed help and advice from other parents. Existing national organisations, such as NCT, Gingerbread, Step Family and Parents Anonymous, started local self-help support groups locally. In addition, new voluntary organisations emerged to offer different forms of support to particular groups of parents, for example, Home Start where one mother befriends another; and Contact a Family where local families whose children have special needs get together.

6. A growing awareness that parenting, participation and involvement don't always come easily but can be learned. Many parents want to know more about parenting and to learn from and share with others. Open University learning groups, Parent Network and Exploring Parenthood workshops have enabled parents to come together around family, child care and parenting issues.

7. A clear government commitment to encouraging voluntary action, parent involvement and self-help in particular. There have been three major government funded initiatives to encourage the development of services and opportunities for child care, self-help and community provision (Opportunities for Volunteering, Under Fives Initiative, Self-Help and Families) amounting to an investment of several million pounds.

The possibilities for parent involvement and partnership, as an individual, in a voluntary organisation, varies from working with a group of children to raising money and employing staff. The rationale for such parent involvement may be the benefits to an individual child or parent; or the benefit to the group of children in having more adults available; or the personal development of the parent; or the organisational development of the playgroup which relies on a parent's availability and activity to keep going. However, there may be significant differences between voluntary organisations employing professionally trained staff, and self-help parent-run groups where the distinction between helper and helped are blurred and the sharing of experience and skills, of mutual advice and support are integral. Equally, the relationship between staff of NSPCC who have statutory duties in the area of child abuse will be different to workers in a family centre which aims to enable and encourage parents to see the centre as their own resource and become actively involved in the running and management.

There are other forms of parent involvement and partnership related to the funding and management of services. Partnerships between local authorities and large voluntary organisations may be varied but essentially professional responsibility and accountability are clear, delivery of services is a contractual matter and fees and funding are negotiated accordingly. It becomes more difficult when local community or parent groups wish to provide a service, such as day care, which is subject to local regulations but where the group relies on the goodwill and support of parents who may have their own priorities and who may lack adequate resources, management expertise, training or support to meet obligations imposed upon them. While the government promotes the concept of partnership between parents and the state and is keen that parents and local groups will provide for themselves, others do not believe that families and communities can or should take over some of the functions of a social services department (Barclay, 1982, para 13.6).

Provision of services for young children through self help and voluntary organisations has often been accused of being appropriate only for the middle class parents with time and resources, skills and experience of dealing with organisations, administration and committees. Clearly, this is a critical factor in determining whether all parents are involved or, indeed, whether what is being provided is appropriate for all parents in an area or the country generally. Johnson (1981) warns that increased participation does not necessarily lead to greater equality (or partnership) and that 'decision makers may be misled into believing that a well-organised minority, pursuing its own interests, is representing the views of the majority'. Gilroy (1982) writing about evolving community-based services also warned of the dangers of building generalised strategies from images of the 'nuclear family'.

Even those parents who are involved and do use the services often require additional support, either at home or within the community (Ferri *et al* 1977). Hadley & McGrath (1980) looking at the development of neighbourhood social services highlighted that families do not live in isolated units but within a pattern of relationships with others who may help or hinder their ability to cope and participate. Shirman (1981) demonstrated that some parents find it difficult to use or participate in any services, even if they are 'on the street corner', while

Finch (1984) argues that it is actually deceitful to promote self-help with working class women, as there is an inherent tension between the self-help element and the provision of pre-school facilities. Equally, Jowett and Sylva (1986) point out that some disadvantaged children may require more intensive resources and educational opportunities such as those of nursery school, rather than group play activities of playgroups, in order to achieve their potential.

There are many critics of self-help, some seeing it as 'a concrete and convenient excuse for avoiding social change' (Henry, 1978), and of parent involvement as a cheap new way of both supporting and policing families by getting 'mothers who can cope to support the ones who cannot' (New & David 1985). De'Ath (1985) identified seven main issues that confronted those parents trying to develop self-help family centres: diversion of time, energy and labour into fund-raising; overextension, the temptation to take on too much; the personal and emotional cost to individuals; the dependence on a pool of non-wage earning people; the limited resources of deprived and disadvantaged areas; the difficulties in recruiting and keeping volunteers; and, recognition that self-help is a participatory process which is complex, time consuming and takes a while to develop and flourish. Many of these factors are equally applicable to parent involvement in provision of other facilities for children under five. Clearly, there are no simple answers. There is some truth in these criticisms, but equally there is ample evidence that parents can be involved in planning, managing and delivering services within the non-statutory sector.

Participation and partnership, as we have argued in chapter 6, is a complex and complicated phenomenon. Just as self-help is both a new organisational type of care as well as a rediscovery of traditional types of community care, so we need to accept that our current services have been failing both parents and young children and we need new principles for change. Van der Eyken (1982) in his evaluation of a befriending scheme Home Start describes this as acknowledging the mother as a potential change agent and building on principles of reciprocity.

To conclude, the arguments for greater involvement in services and for partnership between parents and professionals are broad based and often conflicting, reflecting as they do the professional or ideological base of the service from which they come. It is perhaps not surprising that parent involvement/participation/partnership has come to mean everything and nothing. Are we talking about parents as learners or teachers? Are they buying a service or being asked to finance and run it? Are they consumers, clients or managers? Are they sharing the care of their child with a professional, or being instructed in the fundamentals of child-rearing? Are they being 'empowered' to take control of services, or simply being asked to fill a gap in inadequate state provision? It is in attempting to answer these questions that we shall examine the power-base of the relationship between parents and professionals, and see under what conditions, if any, partnership is possible.

4. Professional or Parent?

Before examining involvement and partnership in more detail, we now consider briefly the question 'what is a professional?' and whether trained workers in the pre-school schemes and services can be described as such. The characteristics of professionalism are described in the literature as a specialised body of skills and knowledge; a prolonged period of training to acquire them; acceptance of the validity of these skills by society at large and therefore the exclusive right to practice them; a professional culture and a code of ethics organised by members of the profession; and a service ethic in relation to clients (Greenwood 1966). Professionals have tended to be self-employed, to rely on the authority of their own professional judgement, and wherever possible to create distance between their own expertise and that of their clients.

A distinction has been drawn by some between full professionals, for example doctors, architects, lawyers and university teachers, and others seen as 'semi-professionals'. Teachers, social workers and nurses are described by Bennett and Hokenstad (1973) as 'people workers', and are seen as being in many respects different in their role and function from the more traditional professionals. Their knowledge base is described as more methodological and less substantive than that of a lawyer or doctor. Their training encourages them to function as catalysts, to communicate information and share insights, attempting to help the client to help himself, rather than simply using their knowledge but not sharing it. 'People worker' professionals are seen less as experts, controlling a body of knowledge, than as transferers of knowledge, developing skills and encouraging change in others.

It is doubtful whether all teachers, social workers or nurses could describe their skills and objectives in this way. There clearly are some people workers who see their role as being to break down the distinction between the trained, qualified professional and the untrained lay person. Community workers, for example, have tended to query the existence of a discrete body of knowledge available only to those with appropriate training, and to stress the validity of everyday experience brought by the families with whom they were working.

> 'If professional status separates a practitioner from his client, if professional training encapsulates an unchangeable body of expertise, if professional qualifications are used to exclude those with fresh knowledge from unconventional backgrounds, community workers in general want none of it'. (Jones and Mayo 1974).

In the pre-school field in particular this approach is beginning to have important repercussions on the development and training of other professionals in their work with families. Most pre-school workers, by virtue of being employed by local authorities, health authorities or voluntary organisations, are not self-employed. But this is not the only respect in which their professional status is in doubt. As Aldrich and Leighton (1985) have pointed out in relation to the teaching profession, teachers are paid employees, with no single union, no control over training, no established code of practice governing their relationship with clients, and answerable to two masters – the Secretary of State on pay, and the local authorities. 'They lack virtually all the attributes whereby aspiring groups have sought to justify their claims to professional status'.

Whilst those with professional training have always enjoyed a position of high status and been held in high regard within society, they have in recent years not been without their critics. Midwinter (1977), for example, in a paper examining the professional-lay relationship as a Victorian legacy, describes the professions as having become

> 'bureaucratised, defensive about manning and function, haunted by false fears of dilution, jittery about evaluation and open accountability, jargon-plagued, status-conscious and sheltering, in a pother of insecurity, behind a barricade of mystique'.

The notion of professionals as creating dependence and disabling their clients has been argued perhaps most forcibly by Illich (1977), and was a central theme in the Court report.

In the pre-school field many of those working with children would consider themselves to be para-professionals or simply parents taking on paid employment. Workers such as playgroup leaders, parent and toddler group workers and childminders for example, queried with the project team where they fitted in to the model of parent-professional partnership. Were they parents or professionals? The study of the

Scottish Pre School Play Association branch in Cumbernauld (**Pugh** *et al* 1987) shows clearly that parents are taking on tasks and responsibilities assumed elsewhere by workers with 'professional' qualifications. In looking at the different roles played by workers and parents in relation to children, we are for the moment including all those who have been trained and are paid to work with other people's children. The chart below summarises some of the key differences in how parents and professionals relate to children. It is based on a paper given by Lilian Katz, Director of the Clearing House of Elementary and Early Childhood Education at the University of Illinois at Urbana-Champaign, USA to a seminar organised by the NCB project in May 1984. It draws on the work of John and Elizabeth Newson (1976) and on a previously published paper (Katz 1982).

	Professionals	Parents
Scope and function	Specific and limited	Diffuse and limitless. Nothing is not the parents business. Parents of young children are never off duty.
Intensity of affect	Low	High emotional involvement leads to more intense inter-action – more anger and discipline, more love and support. Difficulties in 'teaching' own children.
Attachment	Optimum detachment – or detached concern. Need to avoid burn-out	Optimum attachment. Parents optimism about child may be in child's best interests.
Rationality	Optimum rationality. Rational analysis of how to proceed on the basis of knowledge of how children learn and develop.	Optimum irrationality. Someone who is 'crazy about that kid' (Bronfenbrenner).

Spontaneity	Optimum intentionality Activities largely pre-determined and pre-meditated in terms of aims, goals and objectives.	Optimum spontaneity. Danger of parent education programmes which encourage parents to become excessively cerebral.
Partiality	Optimum impartiality. Universalism – must be equally available to each child.	Highly partial. Biased in favour of own children, wanting the best for them.
Responsibility	Concern for all children. Balance response to unique individual with responsibility to group.	Concern with own child. Protect their own children's uniqueness.

Whilst many parents take on roles as workers with other people's children, these very clear distinctions should be borne in mind, particularly in terms of emotional intensity. In stressing parents' roles as their children's main educators and health carers, it is important not to lose sight of this degree of involvement, which as the Newsons (1976) point out gives parents both strength and vulnerability.

All the other caring agencies that we can devise can never be quite as satisfactory as the 'good-enough' parent (to use Winicott's term). The best that community care can offer is impartiality – to be fair to every child in its care. But a developing personality needs more than that: it needs to know that to someone it matters more than other children; that someone will go to unreasonable lengths, not just reasonable ones, for its sake.'

5. The Extent of Partnership and Parent Involvement

Despite the recommendations of most of the major education reports published in the last 25 years, studies suggest that whilst arguments in favour of a closer relationship with parents may have been accepted in theory, there is still some way to go in practice. The national CHES study of 13,000 children under five, for example, found that contrary to popular opinion, less than half of the mothers with children at playgroups had helped in the previous term, and in local authority nursery schools and classes the figure was only 13% (Osborn et al 1984). Day nurseries found difficulty in generating any kind of parental or community activities. Similar findings are reported by Blatchford (1982) in a study of transition from home to nursery school, where less than half the schools encouraged parents to stay and help in the classroom, and even those who did reported that less than one in ten of the mothers actually stayed.

In looking at what determines whether or not a mother becomes involved, Osborn concludes that it 'depends largely on whether or not she believes that her help is needed or welcomed, the degree to which she feels she has sufficient time or the necessary skills to participate, and also perhaps her own demands vis-à-vis her child's attendance at the pre-school institution'. Much therefore depends on the value that the mother places on the involvement, both for herself and for her child, and this will reflect her perception of the school's attitude towards her. The findings of other studies are striking in the unanimity with which they report parents' wishes to be more closely involved in their children's schooling, coupled with a sense of confusion and lack of understanding as to how they should go about it (see for example Tizard 1981, Blatchford 1982, Smith 1980, Filkin 1984, Ferri et al 1981). Parents are described as being 'desperately concerned for their children, uncertain of themselves and their roles, and confused and lacking in confidence about which questions to ask' (Filkin 1984).

Not all parents wish to show their interest by actually working in the centre – many prefer to leave this to the staff whose job they see it to be. Others argue that as children start on the road to independence, they should leave them to make their own way without their parents in attendance. But there can be few parents who would not welcome a greater understanding and sharing of views about the education of their young children. As Smith (*op cit*) concludes in her study of parents in pre-school groups:

> 'We have evidence that parents show considerably greater interest in their children's pre-school experience than the staff in charge of their children's groups appear to take into account. This is a striking waste of potential. Our recommendation is that staff should be willing to recognise parents' interest and exploit and develop it.'

None of the studies cited above appear to have asked either parents or staff to consider the possibility of pre-school care and education being seen as a partnership. At an individual level, it is quite possible that parent and worker may have developed a relationship based on mutual trust and respect, although if levels of involvement reflect the expectations of the centre rather than the wishes of the parents, then this may not happen easily. At a more formal level, about half of the parents in Tizard's study (*op cit*) said they would like to be involved in decision-making. In stark contrast, the teachers in this study did not refer to parents' rights to be either informed or consulted, and certainly did not see parent involvement as a way of enriching parents' lives. Others have found parents to be more interested in the progress of their own children than in the wider affairs of the centre or school, and it seems unlikely that these parents would want to take a management role, any more than the staff would wish them to (Filkin 1984, Watt 1985).

6. Dimensions of Parent Involvement

Our own study was less concerned with numbers of parents in centres than with the different kinds of roles that parents are playing in schools and pre-school centres; with the quality of the relationship between parents and teachers/centre workers; whether this could be defined as a partnership; and with the factors that affect this relationship. But how should partnership be defined? In reviewing studies of parent involvement we found little discussion of the concept of partnership. Gordon (1969), one of the earliest to write on the topic, outlines a five point scale identifying different roles parents might assume:

parents as supporters – service givers, clerical, custodial facilitators, maintenance, fund-raisers;

parents as learners – on parent education courses, observing their children with some explanatory help;

parents as teachers of their own children – taking toys and books to use at home;

parents as teacher aides and volunteers in a classroom – preparing materials, reading stories, working with children;

parents as policy makers and partners – advisory board members.

To these, Smith (1980) added a further category which she found predominant in her Oxford study:

parents as sharers in their children's experiences

A study of 18,000 institutions by van der Eyken (1983) provides another analysis. Initially three categories of involvement were proposed:

support – fund-raising, publicity, and help outside the institution;

participation – actual help given in sessions inside the institution;

control – aspects of management, joint consultation with staff, some liaison with external agencies on behalf of the institution.

A further study of the changing role of day nurseries as part of this sample resulted in van der Eyken (1984) proposing two further categories:

contractual involvement – 'working with parents', where the family is involved only in a compulsory and, perhaps, client-orientated relationship, focusing on family management, cognitive child development, and possibly counselling;

self-initiated and self-generating involvement – where the family uses the resources available in the nursery to enhance their own goals and aims, which may have no direct connection with the institution.

The final category of parents using the nursery for their own purposes, has also been noted elsewhere, for example by Ferri and Niblett (1977) who in their study of disadvantaged parents and playgroups describe a category associated with the groups' 'warmth' – 'the extent to which mothers used the groups as a place where they were able and welcome to spend some time and enjoy social contact with staff and other mothers – simply the opportunity to sit down and relax, have a cup of tea and a chat'. Laishley and Lindon (1980) in their six point outline of parent involvement also include two categories that could be seen more as parent-support than institution-support: **social contacts for parents** and **offering help to parents with their problems.** Both of these are seen as particularly relevant to institutions such as day nurseries which are working with a high proportion of families under stress, or experiencing loneliness and isolation. The growth in the development of adult education activities in infant and nursery schools, and in some family centres, could also be seen as being of more direct benefit to the parents concerned than to the institution itself. However this was usually part of a developing pattern, and was often an essential prerequisite to other forms of involvement.

Within child health services there seemed to be no comparable research that offered definitions of parent-professional relationships within child health clinics, health centres or hospitals. However two papers given to National Children's Bureau study days provided useful definitions. Nicholl (1986) teased out three elements in a relationship based on partnership:

- it must be *equal,* with parents and professionals regarding each other as colleagues and confidants, sharing information, confidences and goals for the child;

- it must be *active,* with both parents and professionals taking an active role in enhancing the child's development, detecting any problems and treating them;

- it must be *responsible,* with both parties taking responsibility for the child's health, but trusting each other and taking risks reliant on the other person's actions.

Davis (1985) offered a framework for co-operation and partnership with parents and children in hospital using the tools of public sector consumerism. These she described as the right to:

information – about the child's medical condition, nature of treatment, hospital procedures, how the ward works, what the rules are etc. This must also be two-way information, nurses need to know what children's food preferences are, what frightens them and so on;

consultation – which takes place before admission and again in the ward about the care plan for the child;

representation – in the planning and managing of individual wards in hospitals and child health services in general;

negotiation – particularly in relation to complaints and redress.

The only typology that made explicit reference to partnership arose from a project in Australia that aimed to enable very poor families to take control of the service (a family centre) by giving them power over the centre's resources. Participation was seen not as a means of involving parents but as the logical outcome of giving power to the families. This is described by Benn (1981) as power over resources, information, decision-making and relationships.

Most of the research described above is derived from roles and relationships between parents and institutions, but it is perhaps more fruitful in examining partnership to look at relationships between an individual parent and a professional worker. The dictionary defines partnership as a 'working relationship between two parties, towards a mutual goal' (OED) or a 'contractual relationship between two or more persons' (Collins). The Warnock report (1978) was the first government report to address the question directly. It states that the relationship between parents and professionals

> should be a partnership, and ideally an equal one . . . For although we tend to dwell upon the dependence of many parents on professional support, we are well aware that the partnership cannot be wholly effective, if at all so, unless it builds upon the parents' capacity to be involved. Thus we see the relationship as a dialogue between parents and helpers working in partnership . . . Professionals have their own distinctive knowledge and skills to contribute to parents' understanding of how best to help their handicapped child, but these form a part, not the whole, of what is needed. Parents can be effective partners only if professionals take notice of what they say and of how they express their needs, and treat their contribution as intrinsically important.'

The Warnock report was, of course, concerned with children with special needs, and it is in the field of special education that the challenge of partnership has been most strongly taken up. Wolfendale (1983) suggests that parents have traditionally been put in the role of 'client' where they are seen as dependent on experts' opinions; passive in the receipt of services; apparently in need of direction; peripheral to decision-making and perceived as inadequate or deficient. If they are seen as partners, however she argues that they are

> 'active and central to decision-making and its implementation; perceived as having equal strengths and equivalent expertise; able to contribute to as well as receive services (reciprocity); able to share responsibility, so that they and professionals are mutually accountable.'

In *Partnership with Parents* Mittler & Mittler (1982) describe the key elements in partnership as mutual respect and recognition of the essential equality between parents and professionals; sharing of information and skills; sharing of feelings; sharing the process of decision-making; recognition of the individuality of families and the uniqueness of the handicapped child. Further, they state:

> Partnership between parents and professionals is justified by the needs of the child, parents and professionals. Each depends on the knowledge, skills and experience of the other if the needs of the child are to be fully met. (p. 49)

This notion of equality if taken out of context can present problems to both parents and professionals. It is important to distinguish between the roles of parents and professionals and not attempt to professionalise parents or diminish professional skills. The important distinction is that of equivalence or, as Davis (1985) puts it 'complementary expertise' where

> 'the expert knowledge of parents on themselves, their aims, their situation generally and their children, complements what the professional has to offer including specialist knowledge and the skills to communicate it.'

Cunningham and Davis (1985) classify relationships between parents and professionals as falling into one of three models. In the **expert model** the professional takes control and makes all the decisions, giving low priority to parents' views and feelings, the sharing of information or the need for negotiation. The approach tends to foster dependency on the part of the parent, who reinforces the expert's power by a reluctance to ask questions. In the **transplant model** the professional recognises the advantage of parents as a resource and hands over some skills (for example training parents in the use of behaviour modification techniques) but they retain control of the decision-making. The **consumer model** assumes that parents have the right to decide and select what they believe is appropriate, and decision-making is ultimately in their control. The foundation of this relationship is one of negotiation and mutual respect, with a more equal balance of power. As Cunningham and Davis point out, a partnership is a contractual arrangement, and as such it is important that the expectations that each party has of each other are made explicit.

As will be explored further in the following chapter, in our own work, we came to define partnership as *a working relationship that is characterised by a shared sense of purpose, mutual respect and the willingness to negotiate. This implies a sharing of information, responsibility, skills, decision-making and accountability.* Whilst there are doubtless many relationships between parents and therapists or psychologists or teachers that fall far short of the ideal or partnership outlined above, it is possible to see why notions of mutual gain, of shared values and assumptions, of shared information, of shared responsibility, and of working towards a shared goal have become central to the debate that followed the 1981 Education Act.

It also raises the question of whether of not partnership is possible when values, assumptions and information are *not* shared, or when the parent is not entitled to discontinue the relationship. In looking at whether partnership is possible within the contractual constraints of work in a day nursery or family centre, for example, Davie (1985) suggests that notions of partnership and interdependence may not be compatible with a professional's statutory responsibility to control the relationship.

7. A Framework For Parent Involvement

During the course of the three year study, these typologies developed by other writers and researchers were assessed in the light of observations made in the 130 nurseries, groups and centres we worked in. Each, though of value, seemed incomplete in itself. In an attempt to focus our own thinking and to help others in the pre-school field to consider their own attitudes and to establish what kind of involvement was appropriate for their own service, we developed the following framework. The framework has been used in the twelve case-studies presented in *Partnership in Action: working with parents in preschool centres* (Pugh *et al* 1987) and also forms part of the training pack produced by the project (De'Ath and Pugh 1986). It is not intended as a blue-print, nor to suggest that there should be a linear progression from non-involvement to ultimate control. Rather, it attempts to present a tool for use by workers in pre-school centres in examining their own work with parents.

1. Non-participation

Parents use a pre-school service purely as a consumer, whether through choice or direction, and do not involve themselves in the way it functions.

  a. active non-participant – a parent who has actively decided not to participate in the centre, for example

  a parent who is working;
  a parent who wants time off from the children;
  a parent who wants to 'buy' professional time.

  b. passive non-participant – a parent who might like to participate but is or feels unable to, for example

a parent who feels the child may not settle if the parent is there;
a parent who lacks confidence, is tired or depressed;
a parent with a limited command of English;
a parent with younger children who may be disruptive.

2. Support

Parents who support the centre from the outside, through practical help or by endorsing the centre's philosophy, for example

fund raising;
providing materials for the centre when asked;
attending open evenings, and social events;
providing moral support, promoting the centre's philosophy;
supporting centre-suggested activities at home.

3. Participation

Parents physically involved in or contributing to the work within the centre, usually under the supervision of the staff, for example

a. Parents as helpers –

servicing the group as a whole;
helping run a particular group or a toy library;
working with children on a rota basis;
going on outings with staff and children;
providing simple nursing care in hospital

b. Parents as learners –

i. about their own child, and the aims of the centre, through attending open evenings, workshops, school assemblies; or sharing children's experiences in the group;

ii. about the wider world, through adult education activities.

4. Partnership

Parents are involved in a working relationship that is characterised by a shared sense of purpose, mutual respect, and the willingness to negotiate. This implies a sharing of information, responsibility, skills, decision-making and accountability, for example

a. Partnership between individual parent and professional for example –

parents as co-workers, co-educators, jointly planning and implementing a programme for their child in the centre or at home;
parents having equal access to information and records;
parents sharing in decision-making for their child;
parents sharing in diagnosis, assessment, planning, review and monitoring of their child.

b. Partnership between parents in general and a particular centre, for example

participation in planning and management;
sharing in formulating aims and objectives, and in planning activities;
sharing in selection of staff;
sharing in selection of children;
evaluation of centre.

c. Partnership between individual parents as workers and a particular centre, for example

visiting homes;
running groups;
counselling other parents;
becoming playgroup leaders and childminders.

d. Partnership between parents and policy makers in the community, for example

through membership of under fives liaison groups, community health councils, PPA regional committees;
through shared information and contacts with district health authorities and education and social service committees.

5. Control

Parents determine and implement decisions, and are ultimately responsible and accountable, either in control of the centre, or of discrete elements within the centre, for example:

selecting, employing and managing staff;
managing resources and budgets;
selecting children;
determining aims and objectives.

The framework includes a wide range of activities that are unlikely to be available in any one centre, and the possibility of more types of involvement or partnership than any one parent could possibly cope with. Nevertheless it has been useful in determining what might be described as the 'partnership proneness' of a pre-school centre or service, and in assessing where the balance of power lies in relationships between workers and parents. It should not be seen as an ideal progression, nor should it be used as a once and for all account of a centre. It is also important to note that partnership or even involvement does not necessarily have to take place within the school or centre, and cannot be measured by the number of parents in a room. Parents who are working, for example, may be involved in the management of a nursery without contributing to the day to day activities. Parents who are closely involved in supporting their children's learning may do so entirely at home.

Two further points need to be made in relation to the framework. One is that it is important to take a centre as a whole and look at what activities staff feel is *appropriate* for parents to be involved in. One nursery, for example, may welcome parents participating in and even planning the daily activities, but not being represented on the management committee. Another may have parents in a majority on the management committee, but not involve parents in the group. A centre may have a welcoming 'open door' policy, but feel that the staff should be wholly responsible for individual children's programmes without any discussion with parents.

Finally, if we compare what *all* parents *actually* do in a centre with what the staff feel it is appropriate for parents in general to do, we may find some interesting discrepancies. The total number who are involved in any way may turn out to be rather smaller than expected, with the same parents participating in a number of different activities. Although there may be nominal participation of parents in planning and management, the one or two involved may not be representative of the whole parent group.

8. Partnership Proneness: Ten Key Factors That Can Help Or Hinder

Partnership, both in theory and in practice, is a complex and elusive concept. As we have described elsewhere (De'Ath and Pugh 1985–6, Pugh *et al* 1987a and b) there are many centres and nurseries with a strong commitment to working with parents, but the relationship between the professionals and parents has seldom achieved the degree of openness and mutual respect that a true partnership requires. Working harder is rarely the appropriate response. Rather, we believe, it is important to consider each centre in terms of ten key factors which appear both to facilitate and hinder any moves towards partnership.

These factors can be divided into three main groups. The first seven points are to do with the nursery or centre itself. Numbers eight and nine are concerned with the skills and attitudes of the staff. The final point reflects the motivation and level of confidence of the parents.

After each section, some questions for discussion have been included. Those who would like to take these questions further are referred to the training pack *Working With Parents* (De'Ath & Pugh 1986)

i. The type, function and overall philosophy of the centre/nursery

The overall aim of the nursery or centre – whether it is intended to complement, supplement or substitute for the care of parents for their children – will have an important effect on the extent to which partnership is possible. A self-help community group, for example, which is concerned to enable local families to take greater control of their own lives, will obviously work with parents in different ways from a day nursery which is intervening in the lives of families whose parenting skills are felt to be in some way inadequate. If, as has been argued, partnership requires a shared sense of purpose and a willingness to negotiate, then the inherent disparity in power between social workers or health visitors on the one hand and parents who have been identified as at risk of abusing their children on the other makes the attainment of such an equal relationship extremely difficult, if not impossible. As McKechnie pointed out, speaking at a project conference on 'partnership with parents; a contract in stress' (*Partnership Paper 6*) it is important to work with such parents towards a shared understanding of what is needed and how this may be achieved, and a shared desire to pursue these goals together.

Our evidence suggests that partnership is easier in centres or nurseries that focus on support rather than intervention, and that offer a community provision open to all local families, rather than a specialist service providing a safety net for vulnerable families. For example, relationships between staff and parents in a nursery class offering pre-school experiences to children are likely to focus on the parent's role in supporting their child's educational development; while in a day nursery many parents may be committed to a contractual arrangement combining a therapeutic programme with activities designed to improve their caring and coping skills. Parents in a support group convened by a member of staff in a hospital neo-natal unit are likely to relate rather differently to the nurses and doctors than parents in a baby and toddler group in the local child health clinic.

We should not assume, however, that particular groups will have a standard approach to working with parents – for example that playgroups will always be more open to parents than schools will. The key factor is how prepared any group or nursery is to work in an open and collaborative way with parents, and how well it is able to respond to the needs of individual children and their families, and to the values and culture of the local community.

Discussion Points

Reviewing the type and function of the centre

* Is the service you offer families

> *complementary* – offering additional social, health and educational opportunities to children similar to those offered by their families, through nursery education, playgroups, nurseries, health visitor check-ups, parent and toddler groups, community centres?

> *supplementary* – offering something extra often to parents and child together, through family centres, nurseries, treatment GP or health visitor, specialist self-help or support groups?

substitute – offering alternative care to children who are severely disabled or ill in hospital, daily care to children of working parents, or foster care (daily or residential) for parents unable to care for their children themselves?

* Does your centre aim primarily to

  alter behaviour and improve parenting skills?
  enable parents to develop skills and confidence?
  discuss all plans with parents from a basis of mutual trust and respect?

* Do you focus primarily on the needs of

  the child
  the parent(s)
  both
  statutory requirements?

* Is the work of your centre problem-focused?

  If so, who determines and resolves the problem?

* Do the aims of the centre reflect

  the views of the professionals, what they think is required?
  the views of the parents, what they find most helpful?

* How easy do local parents find it to use your centre?

  Have you actually asked them?

* Are the days and hours open convenient to parents?

  Have you asked them?

* What opportunities are there for parents

  to comment on how useful they find your centre?
  to suggest changes to existing services?
  to be involved in establishing new services?

ii. Establishing a policy on working with parents

The centres and nurseries in our study were more likely to be working towards partnership with parents if they had an explicit commitment in the form of a policy statement on parent involvement. This needed to operate at two levels: on the part of the local authority or voluntary organisation; and within individual centres or nurseries. Increasingly, local authorities who are devising coherent policies on their provision for children under five are now including parent involvement, and the need to consult parents in planning services, as a central theme of their manifesto (see Pugh 1988). Many of the most innovative centres visited were in local authorities that had stated their commitment to developing work with parents, and were prepared to make some additional funds and support available to enable this to happen.

There can of course be problems with a 'top-down' approach that stems from a centrally devised policy statement without adequate consultation with the grass-roots workers whose job it will be to implement the policy. In some instances, policies requiring fairly drastic changes in the structure of nurseries and the role of staff were devised for laudable reasons (usually intending to provide a service felt to be more appropriate to the needs of the families using it) but were then handed on to staff with little consultation and inadequate opportunities for in-service training. One of the day nurseries studied (Pugh *et al* 1987a, p49) was a case in point, illustrating developments observed in many such nurseries. The social services department had devised a policy encouraging parent involvement, but had not developed any practice guidelines as to how this policy might be implemented, nor had the staff been given any additional time or training to take on a very different and demanding role.

In addition to local authority policy, individual nurseries or centres are more likely to be able to develop their work with parents if a clear statement about the role of parents is included in their aims. Many of the centres visited included statements about 'increasing parents' self confidence' and 'improving parenting skills', but few went as far as Moorland Children's Centre (Pugh *et al* 1987b) which stated that it wished 'to confirm parents in their role as contributors to and consumers of services' and 'to share in the formulation of policy in the nursery'. A confusion over what was expected of parents, of what roles they should play and of what the staff should either ask or expect them to do, was one of the main difficulties encountered. When expectations were made clear – for example a place in the nursery is conditional upon the parent doing five sessions on the rota per term; or a simple contract is devised as the child comes into the nursery and is discussed on a regular three-montly basis with the parent – then parents and workers both seemed to be more satisfied with their own roles. Where there was no clearly defined policy on what both parents and staff are expecting of themselves and each other, it was common to hear workers complain that parents never stayed to work with the children, whereas parents in the same nursery felt that their help was neither needed nor wanted.

Discussion Points

Reviewing and implementing policy statements and practice guidelines on working with parents

* Are there any explicit policy statements on parent involvement or developing work with parents

    by your local authority?
    by your health authority?
    by any of your local voluntary organisations?

* Are there any practice guidelines available for pre-school centres and services on developing work with parents?

* Have pre-school workers and parents been involved in any discussions, or drawing up of policy or guidelines?

* Do the parents you work with know

    about any policy statements on working with parents?
    about any guidelines on how to develop work with them?
    what your aims are with regard to working with them?

---

iii. Management

Management of any pre-school centre, even a small playgroup, can be a time consuming and complex responsibility for parents, especially if they have had no previous management experience. Whether or not parents are entitled to participate in management in ways other than as token representatives will be partly determined by the type of centre: one or two parents acting as managers to encourage parent involvement in a centre is very different from parents taking full financial and legal responsibility, and being fully accountable for the centre.

With the exception of playgroups and some community groups, parents were fully involved in management in very few of the centres studied. Many of the parents questioned did not appear to be interested in total management responsibility, particularly when their lives were already busy with the demands of bringing up small children, and indeed many of the parent governors were parents whose children had passed the pre-school stage and felt they had a bit more time on their hands. Even when parents were not themselves interested in management, however, they did welcome the existence of parent representatives who would take forward concerns on their behalf.

A number of issues were identified in those centres which had begun to involve parents more fully in management. These can be summarised as:

a. the need to clarify the roles, tasks and responsibilities of management committees – where does the power actually lie, which decisions can the management committee make and which are made elsewhere? As Eisenstadt (1985) points out, 'staff and parents must be clear about the parameters of user control, which issues are genuinely negotiable and which are not; and staff must be honestly willing and able to share decision-making and to carry out decisions they may have opposed'.

b. problems related to access to records and to confidentiality, when parents are involved in discussing matters related to other families in their local community;

c. the importance of developing strategies to enable parents to participate in management, and of providing training and support for them. Few parents in the centres studied would have had the confidence to put themselves forward for the management committee, had they not first participated in and been supported by groups and other activities in the schools or groups their children attended (see for example, Lynncroft Primary School, Pugh *et al* 1987b). Having put their names forward, there were still many obstacles to full participation. The meetings were conducted in language that was often jargon-ridden. Parents' views did not appear to be encouraged or valued. It was not always easy to put items on the agenda. Meetings were not at times that made attendance easy – they coincided with children's bedtimes and went on late into the evening. Child care facilities were seldom available. And there were few opportunities for preparation or training. One interesting initiative in respect of this latter point was a scheme in Moorland Children's Centre (Pugh *et al* 1987b) where prospective office holders on the committee 'shadowed' the current chair, secretary and treasurer for several meetings before taking office themselves.

d. whether or not the staff feel that parents are able and willing to become involved in management. Woodchurch Family Support Project for example is described as 'having narrowly defined management functions and a formal management style', and being 'too high powered for parents'. It is not perhaps surprising therefore that the coordinator is 'pessimistic' about change in management context and format' or that project workers and the management committee 'profess a desire to involve parents in management yet seem not to believe that this is possible' (Pugh *et al* 1987a).

e. The question of potential conflict between parents and professionals when the views of the parents are at odds with those of the staff; for example, on whether or not the centre should employ male child care workers, or how and when children should begin to learn to read. In few of the centres studied had parents reached this level of confidence, but it was beginning to happen, and with changes in legislation leading to greater parent representation on managing bodies, this could become a real test of what is meant by partnership.

Discussion Points

Parents and Management

* Where and with whom does power and management responsibility lie in your scheme

> for ultimate financial and legal accountability?
> for the overall effective running?
> for the day to day running?

* Who is involved in decisions about any of the following

> policy on aims, objectives, priorities
> selection and working conditions of staff
> admissions policy for children
> opening hours
> charges
> changes in main services, additional activities?

* What opportunities currently exist in your scheme for parents

> to be involved in the role of parent managers?
> to be actual parent managers?

* What is, or would be, the purpose for such opportunities

    for parents?
    for the staff?
    for the children?
    for the community?

* What training/support/apprenticeship is available?

* How are management meetings arranged?

    Are the time, agenda and language accessible?
    How are decisions made, agreed, recorded?

* In a committee of shared management what would be the differences in the roles, tasks and membership functions

    of parent members?
    of staff members?
    of other members?

* How do parents raise issues with

    a) Staff
    b) Management

    Through informal conversations?
    Regular explicit formal or informal opportunities?
    Representation to management committee?
    Representation to a higher authority?

iv. Funding

The question of resources, or lack of them, dominated our deliberations on working with parents. Services for children under five are given a low priority both nationally and locally, and in many parts of the country the issue is whether there are any nursery classes or day nurseries at all, rather than the quality of the relationship between parents and professionals within them. Although working with parents in new ways is principally about changing attitudes, perceptions and styles of service, there is no doubt that if staff are to take on responsibilities and tasks in addition to their work with children, then this is considerably facilitated if there are adequate staff, equipment, premises and resources. For example, three of the schools in the study – Lynncroft, Woodlands and Walkergate – had been able to build or adapt rooms or centres specifically for their work with parents, and to employ a member of staff to develop this aspect of their work. Whilst excellent work was observed where teachers were involving parents in groups with their children with no additional help, activities such as visiting parents at home and setting up parent and toddler groups and adult education classes are difficult for any worker to undertake on top of a full-time commitment to a group of small children.

Additional funding for work with parents was sometimes made available through local authority budgets as part of their stated policy on encouraging parent involvement. More often than not, other sources of revenue had been tapped, including Urban Aid, inner city partnership, joint finance, voluntary agencies and charities, the Manpower Services Commission and the DHSS Under Fives Initiatives. Although such funding supported the development of many exciting initiatives, there are major disadvantages in using short-term funding. Schemes such as Home from Home (Pugh *et al* 1987b) and many playgroups (PPA, 1987) which have relied heavily on MSC funding are only able to employ workers for a maximum of one year. The constant turnover of staff unsettles parents and children alike and imposes heavy burdens on the few permanent staff who are responsible for supervision and training. For centres funded in whole by a short-term grant – for example by the Under Fives Initiative – there is the difficulty of securing permanent funding after the initial two or three period, a quest which has imposed considerable strains on many centres' leaders (van der Eyken, 1987).

Many pre-school centres work extensively with parents at no additional cost by using parents either as volunteers or as workers on very low wages. Whilst playgroups and other community groups are often cited as excellent examples of the virtues of parent involvement, and of parents being able to set up and run their own groups, many such groups do labour under considerable hardship, relying on small grants (if they can get them), on the fees paid by parents using the group, on an endless round of fund raising events, (£7 million raised by PPA groups in 1987) and on the fact that playgroup leaders are usually prepared to work in the group for a nominal hourly wage. For many families today, survival depends on the woman earning rather more than playgroups are able to pay; and for women who are working, time spent on the playgroup rota can be an expensive luxury. Elsewhere in the voluntary sector, the insecurity of funding experienced by many community groups means that much of the energy of key workers is expended on seeking further funds rather than on providing the services needed by children and families.

Shortage of funding nationally for services for children under five means that many pre-school workers are parents, volunteers or paraprofessionals rather than professionals as such. This study has show that the involvement of parents in centres as workers and contributors rather than just as passive recipients, has a great deal to recommend it. Countless parents have grown in confidence and have developed skills as they have taken on new roles, and the centres have benefited from their help and their increased understanding. But it is important that parents are not exploited and used as 'cheap labour', providing services at a much reduced cost and thus relieving the pressure on hard-pressed local authorities.

Discussion Points

Ensuring adequate and appropriate funding and use of resources.

* Is there a commitment locally to develop services for families with children under five?

> How do you know?
> What types of funding are available?
> Is there any joint planning between health, education and social services?
> Is there any joint planning between the voluntary and statutory sectors?
> Is there a family fund?
> Is there an under-fives liaison officer?

* How much funding is made available to voluntary groups providing facilities for under fives?

> Is it adequate to provide the range of facilities needed?
> Is it sufficient to provide for the numbers of under fives?
> Is it sufficient to provide stability and long term planning?
> Is it sensitive to minority groups – working parents, black And ethnic minority groups, special needs of children or parents?

* Is funding allocated along fixed criteria:

> for which groups may apply?
> for the type of provision that is acceptable?
> to develop services in response to local need?

to replicate existing provision
to provide pump-priming for innovative schemes?
to maintain existing services?
to extend or expand existing services?

* Is there an assumption that parents will be involved:

    as workers or helpers? is this seen as 'cheap labour?'
    as managers or governors? is this accountability or tokenism?
    in undertaking tasks that should be the responsibility of statutory services?
    in discussing funding, budgeting, use of resources?

* Are you taking full advantage of resources available to you:

    through joint funding and planning with health, education, social services?
    through seeking traditional funding specifically to develop and promote work with parents?
    through releasing or re-allocating resources in your centre to develop work with parents, a part-time post for example?

* Funding requirements can help or hinder:

    Exactly what requirements are made for you?
    How can you use these to your advantage e.g. monitoring and evaluation?
    If they are inappropriate, how can you relay that to the sponsors?
    If they are designed to be supportive, are you getting the best value for them, e.g. training, supervision, reports, visits, financial monitoring?

v. Location and premises

Where a centre is, whether it is accessible to local families and to those who have to come by public transport, and how welcoming the premises are, are all factors that affect whether parents come to the centre at all and, having arrived, feel inclined to stay. The schools, nurseries, family centres and playgroups in the study ranged from brand new purpose-built centres to old church halls and leaking portacabins, but the age and state of the surroundings seemed less important than whether or not parents were made to feel at home when they got there.

Initial appearances can often deter a nervous newcomer, and some schools in particular seemed designed to keep parents out, with a myriad of doors opening off the playground and no obvious signs as to where the main entrance was. Parents responded well to clear signs (in different languages where appropriate) which welcomed them and pointed to the reception area or parents room. Having some space that was 'theirs', where they could make a cup of coffee and chat to friends was also important. Shortage of space is one of the main difficulties facing staff wishing to develop work with parents and most of the centres visited were bursting out of the space allocated them. Some had been able to put up portacabins in the playground or on nearby wasteground, some had been able to take over empty classrooms, or use part of a corridor or – in some cases – were using the staff room.

If parents are able to have a base for their own groups, and are sometimes able to invite professionals to join them on their terms this may go some way towards reducing the distance between them and professionals, and minimise the feeling of powerlessness felt by some parents. The value of working on parents' 'territory' rather than in professionals' clinics and offices has also led to the development of many community-based and home-based schemes. Approaches such as educational home visiting schemes and the Portage project, in which teachers and psychologists work with parents in their own homes and develop a programme tailor made to the needs of the individual child, provide an excellent opportunity for a partnership which accepts that both parties have an equally valid contribution to make.

Discussion Points:

Making the best of your location, premises and space.

* How easy is it for parents to use your centre:

   How far do they have to come?
   Is there a local bus?
   Do the days and times of parent activities fit in with bus and school collecting times?
   Do your parent activities clash with others in the area?

* How welcoming is your centre when parents arrive:

   Is there a welcoming message?

Are there directions to different rooms or activities?
Are signs written in different languages?
Do you have photos of the staff with their names?
Is it bright, colourful and cheerful?

* How are parents looked after when they arrive:

Is there 'parent' space for coats and shopping?
Is there somewhere to sit for coffee or tea?
Does someone 'look after' visitors and new parents?
Can parents sit and chat or do they go straight to groups or activities?

* Is your centre inappropriate for some parents, for example:

The location in the community, e.g. too far, difficult journey?
The type of building, e.g. too many stairs?
Lack of space, e.g. for prams, for adult sized chairs?
Lack of rooms e.g. for parents room, quiet room, group room?

* Could you make better use of the space you have by:

dividing up large rooms?
utilising cupboards, corridors, entrance halls, cloakrooms?
annexing other people's space or rooms nearby?
extending into outside play areas or wasteground?
planning activities in different ways to involve parents?

* Could you develop work with parents somewhere else:

In parent's homes?
In other community settings e.g. health clinics?
By setting up out-reach groups, activities or a parents centre?
By linking with other professionals, workers and parents?

vi. Time

It is easy to underestimate the amount of time taken to begin to change the attitudes and expectations of parents and professionals, and begin to work towards more open relationships. One school visited in the study said it had taken 12 years of planning to set up a parents centre and begin to establish parents groups. All the centres described (Pugh *et al* 1987 a, b) point to the time taken by parents to develop the confidence to undertake new roles. With the current interest in parent involvement, many schools have been tempted to invite parents into the classroom or to set up a group without thinking through either why they wanted to do it or what they – or the parents – might get out of it. These are perhaps the people who have said plaintively 'Well, we set up a meeting/open evening/parents group, but no one came'.

The experience of the schemes we visited suggests that time is needed:

- to think through carefully and discuss WHY parent involvement is important before developing any new approaches or involving parents in new ways:

- to talk with parents about their expectations and understanding of involvement, and WHAT they would want;

- to visit other schemes and centres which are already working with parents and LEARN from their successes and mistakes while remembering that no two centres are the same and that parents may want different things;

- to PERSUADE other professional colleagues that what you are planning to do is important and could benefit them as well;

- to SET UP new activities and approaches which are likely to be over and above the everyday requirements of your job;

- to ENABLE the work to develop at its own pace (both for staff and for parents);

- to RESPOND to the needs of parents and the skills and interests of the staff, rather than seek to meet the requirements of a pre-determined blue-print;

- to ENABLE parents to grow and develop at their own pace and not be rushed into activities, group roles or responsibilities before they are ready;

- to REVIEW constantly how the programme is going, ask parents and staff for feedback, take note of what they say and negotiate and make changes where appropriate;

- to PROVIDE staff and parents with appropriate (and regular) training and support as they take on new activities and roles.

Discussion Points

Planning and Managing Time As a Key Successful Partnership

- Have you allowed enough time to:

    discuss why parent involvement is important?
    discuss what parent involvement means?
    discuss what parents want?
    visit other schemes and centres?
    learn from others successes and mistakes?
    persuade colleagues this is important?
    set up new activities?
    try out new approaches?
    let things work at their own pace?
    respond to needs, skills and interests?
    enable individuals to develop at their own pace?
    review how things are going?
    consider any feedback?
    re-negotiate with parents and staff?
    introduce changes or modification?
    provide training?
    provide support?

vii. Method and strategies

The framework presented in chapter 7 suggests that there are many ways in which parents and professionals are working together, and that a range of methods and strategies are required if all parents are to be reached. As Pen Green expressed it (Pugh *et al* 1987a) 'Parents relate to the centre according to their own needs and at their own pace'. The key factors that emerged from all the centres studied were

- the need for flexibility in responding to the changing needs of local families;

- the importance of a choice of activities to enable parents to become involved at the point that suited them as individuals;

- opportunities within the centre for individuals to grow and to move on from shy observer to participant to partner.

It is the *process* of this development that lies at the heart of decisions over which methods to use, and it is this that the case studies attempt to portray. As Laishley (1985) has said

'The essence of good practice in parent involvement is not so much the programmes of action, but how people have reached the decision about what they will do and exactly how they carry out the programme'.

It is not possible here to look at the range of methods that centres might consider, and some are in any case covered in previous sections. A few are selected as being particularly important;

a. written communications – in language (whether English or their mother tongue) that parents can understand; including both regular newsletters and a brochure outlining the aims of the centre and the role that parents might play; and perhaps a home-nursery diary of regular communication about what has happened during the day

b. personal contacts between staff and parents – individual interviews with all parents before a child starts at the centre; home visits for those who find coming to the centre difficult; opportunities for informal discussion on a daily basis, and more formal sessions at regular intervals, to share information and review progress.

c. informal contracts or agreements between parent and centre, reviewed at regular intervals, establishing what the parent and the worker each expect of the child's time in the nursery and what their respective roles are.

d. making the centre welcoming – clear notices, space that is the parents' own, clarity about how parents fit into the daily routine.

e. opportunities to participate in children's learning – discussion about the centre's aims and objectives and the programme of work with the children; invitations to become involved in specific tasks.

f. something for parents – a cup of coffee, somewhere to relax, adult education classes, parents groups – and crèche facilities to enable them to take advantage of the classes.

g. participation in the centre – parents taking turns on the rota, helping with out-of-school activities, sharing their skills in the classroom, running the toy library.

h. partnership in the centre – sufficient information to be able to contribute to a discussion on their own child with confidence and understanding, feeling that the professional concerned is listening to and taking account of their point of view.

i. parents as workers – as home visitors, as counsellors, as playgroup leaders, as childminders.

j. training opportunities to enable parents to develop the skills required both to undertake those tasks, and to participate in management.

k. parents as evaluators – asking parents for feedback on the centre and how it is meeting their needs or those of their children.

l. working parents – ways of enabling the involvement of parents who may not be able to attend during the day.

Discussion Points

Identifying appropriate strategies.

a. *Non-participation* of some parents was described earlier as being either active or passive.

   - Consider some of the parents who do not attend your centre and identify why you think this might be so.

   - Consider whether any of the following ideas might encourage those parents to attend.

   - How could you find out from the parents which strategies might be helpful or appropriate for their needs?

   - How do you plan to respond to the needs of parents from different racial, religious and cultural backgrounds?

b. *Support* strategies for involving parents in supporting the centre from outside are the most common. It is important to remind yourself of what you are already doing since many of these activities can also be used to encourage participation in the centre itself.

---

* How frequently do you involve parents in any of the following:

   fundraising?
   supplying materials (newspapers, egg boxes)?
   social events, open evenings?

* Is it some parents, or all parents, who are asked, encouraged or invited to do any of the above?

c. *Participation*

* Have you considered ways of improving communications and building up trust between parents and staff?

   Is the centre welcoming, and easy for parents to find their way around?
   Is there written information for parents about the centre, to give to parents before their child starts?
   Are there newsletters, leaflets, posters in different languages if appropriate, but always free of jargon.
   Do you have a noticeboard for parents, or photographs of staff?
   Can you make personal contacts – visiting families at home, arranging social events at the school, involving parents in outings with the children.
   Is there a parents/users group?

* Are parents able to understand the aims and objectives of your work, and what you are offering their child?

   Can parents stay until their child has settled into the centre?
   Are there regular discussions with every parent, and opportunities to discuss what is going well, as well as any problems?
   Do you organise open evenings and parent workshops?
   Are parents able to come to some assemblies?
   Are there displays of work and photographs on the walls describing particular projects or pieces of work and what children are learning from them?
   Do clinics and health centres share information on health matters?

* Are parents aware of their own educational role?

   Is this made clear in the activities above?
   Are there books and games for parents to use with their children at home?

* In what ways are parents able to participate in the centre?

> Is there a range of activities from which to choose, to enable parents to opt in where they feel comfortable?
> Do all the ideas come from the staff?
> Can parents initiate activities?
> Do you give specific invitations, rather than just saying 'come in any time you want'?
> Can they help on the rota?
> Can they share their skills, knowledge and experience with the children and staff?
> Can they work with small groups of children, or with their own child?
> Can they help run a toy library, or the Christmas bazaar, or a parent and toddler group?

* Are there opportunities to meet parents own needs?

> Is there a parents room, or somewhere they can make a cup of tea?
> Are there adult education classes?
> Are there discussion groups and coffee mornings?
> Is there information and advice for parents, and counselling if it is needed?

d. *Partnership*

* Do parents have access to information about their children?

> Are they entitled to keep their own child's health record?
> Are these records used as a basis for discussion between health professionals and parents?
> Do parents have access to school/centre records?
> May they comment on them or contribute to them?
> Why are the records kept? Are staff and parents clear about the reasons?
> Do parents have sufficient information to contribute to decisions about special educational placement, medical treatment etc?

* Are parents able to share in discussion about the curriculum of the centre, or the programme for their own child?

> How sensitive are you to what parents are doing at home with their children?

* Are parents involved in developmental checkups and reviews?

* Are staff clear about what parents want the centre to provide for their children, and are parents clear about this and about their role?

    Are there regular opportunities to look at expectations?
    How easy is it to find time to listen to parents?
    Are parents and staff clear about opportunities that exist for partnership?
    Are rights and responsibilities clearly defined?

* Are parents encouraged to become involved in the management of the centre, and is appropriate training and support available?

    Who makes the decisions (see section on management).
    If there is no management committee, might a user committee be a first step to involving parents?

* Are there some strategies suggested above that would not be appropriate for parents to share in?

    because of centre policy?
    because of staff views?
    because parents don't want to?
    Who makes the decisions about whether or not parents can share in these activities?

e. *Parents as workers*

* Have you been able to share any of your skills with parents?

* Have you been able to share the skills that parents are able to offer?

* Have the opportunities been created for parents to contribute as workers to the scheme as a whole or to support other parents?

* Has the necessary training and support been provided?

* Are parents being adequately rewarded financially for their contribution to the scheme?

f. *Partnership in the community*

* Are there places for parents on local and regional policy-making committees?

* How are parents selected to fill these places?

* What strategies are there for ensuring that the parent members of committees represent the widest possible view?

* How easy is it for parents to get to meetings, and to understand and to participate in the discussion once they are there?

* Is there training and support available to parents who wish to take on these commitments?

* Is the parents' role and the purpose of their participation clear to all members of the committee.

viii. Changing Professional Roles, Developing New Skills and Looking at Attitudes

The changing emphasis of work in the pre-school field means that many of those who trained to work with young children are now finding themselves working with parents as well. This change has implications for the skills required of professionals as they take on new roles, and for how professionals and parents view each other. As 'parent power' has grown, so some workers have feared that their professionalism will be undermined and diminished. The breaking down of barriers has led some workers to feel that greater familiarity with parents may breed contempt. This has not been our experience. On the whole, workers have found that as they have become more open and have shared their skills more readily with parents, so this has enhanced rather than reduced their own and parents' perceptions of their professional role.

The key shift in role has been to move away from always being a fixer of problems/teacher of skills/imparter of knowledge/healer of ills towards enabling and facilitating parents to develop some of these skills themselves. For many workers this facilitating role will be combined with a continuing commitment to teach or heal, and for some it may cause some confusion. This is perhaps particularly true of health visitors and social workers as they attempt to combine friendly advice and support with those elements of control and coercion required by their role as watchdogs of the state. It is clearly important that if roles are to be redefined they are also clarified, so that both workers and parents know what to expect of each other. Sudden changes in one centre run by a national voluntary organisation for example, where a decision had been made at head office that staff should support rather than run groups, led to staff saying that they felt powerless and undervalued and the parents took some time to use the considerable skills of the staff as a resource.

What skills were found to be important? The authoritarian approach of many professionals suggested that a special emphasis should be put on the willingness to share skills, to listen to what parents have to say, to be non-judgemental and non-dogmatic, and to be clear about one's own values but able to work with those whose values and attitudes may be different. Another important skill, and one that was missing in a number of centres as they concentrated on developing work with parents, was the ability to balance the needs of children against those of their parents, and to ensure that the quality of the work with children did not suffer. At a more basic level, we found that political astuteness and the ability to persuade local politicians to support new initiatives with hard cash was important, and as one health visitor put it 'You need a sense of humour, and if you can manage on no sleep, so much the better!

And finally, attitudes, for new skils and strategies will bear little fruit unless professionals really want to develop a partnership with parents, and support the notion of a shared sense of purpose, mutual respect and a willingness to negotiate. Whilst only a small minority of parents wished to be involved in management, all wished to be valued for what they could offer, listened to and taken seriously. A recurring theme throughout this study has been of the conflict between those approaches which are working towards this end, and those which are in some way attempting to change parents' behaviour, either by improving skills in which parents are felt to be deficient, or by developing parents' capacity to teach their own children. Unless such intervention can be embarked on within the spirit of negotiation and dialogue, then such approaches can hardly be viewed as a partnership.

Even in the most open of centres, it appeared difficult to move away from an imbalance of power between parents and staff. As Naomi Eisenstadt (1985) argues in her paper on parents and professionals sharing management at Moorland, it is only too easy for staff to present an issue as an area in which parents can make decisions, and yet the professional is only prepared to accept one option. This is as true for questions about curriculum, about admissions, about information, as it is about management – where ultimately does the power lie, and what can and cannot be negotiated and shared? The key figure in encouraging the development of attitudes conducive to partnership was the head of the centre or nursery. The head's role in choosing staff, in developing policy, and in creating an ethos supportive to the development of partnership was crucial. As far as other members of the team were concerned, centres which experienced particular difficulties were those in which staff had been drafted into new situations with no additional training – for example staff from day nurseries having to develop skills in working with parents, as their day nursery became a family centre, often overnight. Centres in which the staff had been selected by the head because they supported the underlying philosophy of the centre were obviously at a considerable advantage in this respect. We were also struck by the number of professionally trained workers who attributed much of what they had learned about working with parents to their experience working in their own children's playgroups.

Discussion Points

Roles, skills and attitudes

* How has your personal experience of being parented and/or being a parent affected how you work with parents?

* What do you feel has been most valuable to you in preparing you to work with parents?

* In what ways, if at all, have staff roles in the scheme or centre changed?

* If staff have a professional training, do they feel that this change has undermined or enhanced their role?

* What are the constraints on this change of role?

* If staff are working as 'parents' advocates', has this created conflict within the scheme or service? If so, how has it been resolved?

* Are parents and staff clear about staff roles?

* Is working with parents an integral part of the role of all those in the scheme or centre?

* What skills do you feel are required to work with parents?

* Are there any that you feel you would like to develop further in yourself?

* How could you go about doing this?

* What do you think you can learn from parents?

* In working towards more open relationships with parents, where does the ultimate power lie and what can be negotiated?

  Who decides admissions policies?
  Who decides what information should be available?
  Who decides what roles parents can play in the centre?
  Who decides on the content/curriculum of the centre?

ix. Training, Support and Supervision

New roles and new skills suggest new approaches to training, yet the overwhelming feedback from the centres visited during the project was that staff were frequently hampered by lack of support and understanding of what they were trying to do, and felt that their initial training prepared them inadequately for a changing professional role. In respect of teachers at least, this view is supported by a study of initial teacher training (Atkin and Bastiani 1985) which found that one third of primary school teachers had little or no preparation for working with parents, and that home-school relations were seen as very marginal in most colleges, reflecting the fact that teachers' work with parents is an 'optional extra' rather than an integral part of their job. The development of a training resource pack (De'Ath and Pugh 1986) for use in multi-disciplinary groups, and the provision of in-service courses became an important part of the project teams' work, particularly in its emphasis on bringing together workers from different backgrounds to learn from each other.

Levels of support and supervision for the staff working in the centres were also found to be an important determinant of how well the work was developing. The centres experiencing the highest levels of stress were those which were having to change the emphasis of their work (for example nursery schools in areas where there were no day nurseries, having to provide social work support for families), with little or no support from local authority advisers.

The key role of the head has already been noted, and nowhere is this more important than in the arrangements made for staff meetings and individual staff supervision. Almost without exception, the centres where parents had the best relations with staff were those in which staff met together regularly as a team, and developed a joint approach to working with each other and with parents. Staff were enabled to share their skills and expertise, and learn from each other and from the parents. As Benn (1981) says 'The way the staff team works together should be a demonstration to the families about how we can work with them . . . until we can care and share with each other we will be unable to do so with the families'.

Regular meetings for all staff are obviously easier in some centres than in others. Combined nursery centres and day nurseries, for example, tend to work a shift system and may find difficulty in getting all staff together at the same time. Some centres are able to close for half a session a week or a month for staff training, whilst those providing full day care would find this more difficult. And the teachers' industrial action during the course of this project prevented any staff meetings at all in some schools.

Nevertheless, good examples of staff support and team work were found in every type of pre-school service, proving that if the centre head felt this to be a high enough priority, time could be found.

Discussion Points

Training, support and supervision

* What are the main training needs in your centre?
  How can they best be met?

* Is there an advisor or consultant with special responsibility for supporting your work with parents?

* Do all staff meet regularly to discuss aspects of the centre's work, including work with parents?

* Are the staff working well as a team?
  Are the staff able to share their skills with each other?

---

x. Parents: attitudes, expectations and roles.

Finally, what of parents, and what does partnership look like from their point of view? No two parents, no two children, are the same nor will they have the same needs, nor will those needs remain constant over a period of time. Most of the centres recognised that it was important to treat parents as individuals with individual needs, and to guard against assumptions such as one frequently heard during the project – "Of course, you'd never get parents like that in here, they're not interested in their children's progress". We met no parents who were not interested in their children's progress, though there were many factors that prevented them becoming as involved in the centre as the nursery workers may have liked. One of these was quite simply whether or not they were working. Many of the assumptions upon which arguments for greater parent involvement are based presume that parents will be free, willing and able to take on the various roles identified by the project. Yet as Scott and Hill (1986) have pointed out, a strategy (such as that in Strathclyde) which sees the active involvement of parents as critical to its success, may fail to recognise that changes in family patterns mean that many working class women have to work to keep their earnings above the official poverty line.

Parents' attitudes towards and expectations of involvement varied, although most, as one might expect, were more interested in working with their own child than in the greater good of the centre as a whole. The crucial factor seemed to be one of choice – not all parents wished to share professional tasks, but the options for greater participation needed to be there. They also wanted information as a basis for discussion, and to be listened to and taken seriously. In summary, the factors that affected parents' attitudes towards the extent and type of participation they would wish for were:

a. whether or not they felt that their help was needed, or whether the workers appeared to be fully in control and happier without any additional adults;

b. whether they felt sufficiently confident about the skills that they had to offer, and felt that they would be valued;

c. whether the task was one that parents felt should be left to the professionals;

d. what other demands there were on their time;

e. whether they felt that their presence would distract their child;

f. whether any direct benefit could be perceived to parent or child;

g. whether they were clear about their role in the group;

h. whether they felt that by pursuing a particular issue of concern, they might be seen as being over-anxious and might alienate members of staff, to the detriment of their own child's progress

i. whether by working in the group, the staff would be 'spying' on them and making observations about their parenting abilities.

A central focus of the study was the different roles parents were playing in pre-school centres, and one of the key issues to emerge was that of reciprocity. Rather than being passive recipients of professional expertise, as has so often been the case, most parents were contributing to the care and education of their own children and were often supporting other parents as well. Their roles were many and various:

supporters – of nurseries and centres and of their own children
teachers – of their own and sometimes others' children
leaders – of parent and toddler groups and playgroups
counsellors of other parents
home visitors
writers of discussion material and information leaflets
carers of their sick children
interpreters for other parents
observers – of children
managers – of centres
planners – of curriculum, of social events
fund raisers – for centres
consumers – of services
trainers
And no doubt many others.

Many of these roles encroached on territory that had traditionally been the preserve of the professional, and it was important for tasks to be clarified, and for rights and responsibilities to be clearly understood. It was also important that parents were not made to feel under undue pressure to take on roles that they felt unable or unwilling to accept. Staff may have to ensure a balance between enabling parents to take on responsibility, whilst not making demands that are too heavy. This was reflected in the report of the Liverpool playgroup which decided after three years of looking at how the group should run that 'the playgroup belongs to local parents. Some bring their children to be looked after. Some look after the others' children. Both groups are equally important'.

And finally to return to the theme of parents' levels of confidence and

and their individual growth. One of the most common reasons given by parents for not becoming involved in their child's pre-school centre is lack of confidence in the face of professional expertise. Shinman (1981) found that as many as a quarter of parents with children under five were not using local services and that 'even if financial resources were available to provide free and splendidly flexible institutionalised provision, the hoped-for goal of reaching over-stretched mothers who lack confidence would not be achieved'. All the centres described (Pugh *et al* 1987a and b) were notable for the strategies that they had devised for reaching out to parents who found it difficult to take that first step through the door or who, having come one, were too nervous to return. The key factors in their success appeared to be the variety of activities on offer, and their ability to begin working from the point at which they were at rather than imposing ideas that may have been professionally acceptable but had little relevance to the parents' own needs. The study of Pen Green for example (Pugh *et al* 1987) showed how four parents gradually became involved in quite different ways, after initially feeling that they didn't 'belong' at all. One parent felt most confident working with small children and started working in the nursery. Another had a small baby and was most at home in the family drop-in centre. A third found that her sewing skills were needed for making Christmas stockings. And a fourth found a sense of purpose in raising money for the Ethiopian famine appeal.

The other point that emerged clearly from the case studies was that of growth, providing there are opportunities for parents to channel energies into new areas of development, and support and encouragment from staff as they do so. In looking at the list of tasks above, it is easy to forget that parents who become managers and decision-makers and playgroup leaders are not always confident middle-class parents with experience of committee procedures and negotiation skills. Many were referred to centres because of the problems they faced as they struggled to bring up their children. Few would have dreamt when they made their first tentative approaches to the centre that they would become such pillars of the local community.

Discussion points

Parents' perspectives

* Have you asked parents what they would like from the centre?

* Do you tend to work mainly with the more highly motivated parents?

* How well do you know the personal circumstances of parents that may affect their involvement in the centres?

* If parents are unable to participate in the centre during the day, are there other opportunities for them to establish good relationships with staff and share in making decisions regarding their children?

* What ways have you found of involving fathers as well as mothers in the centres?

* Are parents able to choose the way in which they relate to the staff and to the centre? Do you think choice is important?

* Do you feel that parents have a right to opt out, or a responsibility to opt in? Are the rights and responsibilities of parents and professionals negotiable? Are they clearly understood?

* Are there some parents who are reluctant to participate in the centre?
  Why do you feel this is?
  What if anything can be or should be done to encourage them to participate?

* How do staff attempt to balance parents' own needs, with their wish for parents to be involved with their children's care and learning?

* Do parents wish to be involved in making decisions about their own child?

* Do they wish to be involved in management?
  Have you asked them?

* What roles are parents able to play in your scheme/centre?
  Are there any that you may think are inappropriate?

* Is it clear to parents and workers what tasks are to be done and by whom?

* If parents take on roles as workers, how does this affect their relationship with other parents, and with workers?

* What training and support is available to enable parents to take on new roles?

9. Conclusion

Over the last ten years, there have been considerable developments in pre-school services in Britain in terms of parent involvement and in a growing awareness that the changing relationship between parents and professionals brings rights and responsibilities to both parties. This study has started from a recognition of the expertise that both parent and professional bring to the care and education of young children, and has looked at ways in which this expertise can be shared in the best interests of all concerned, but most particularly the children. It has looked at concepts of parent involvement, family support, participation and non-participation, consumer involvement and partnership, both in pre-school centres around the country and in the research literature. We have to conclude that partnership as such is still far from a reality in most pre-school settings.

Partnerships of any kind are complex. In the current economic climate, when most services for under fives are discretionary and many are vulnerable to cut-backs in public expenditure, partnerships between parents and professionals have to be seen in the context of other, broader partnerships – between statutory and voluntary agencies, and between central and local government. Issues related to parent power and active citizenship are not necessarily compatible with a genuine partnership between *all* parents and those who work in and run the services they and their children use. Not all parents have the information, the resources or the power to participate in the partnership. Not all parents wish to be more involved, and not all professionals either know how to or are willing to work in partnership.

In looking at the roles of parents and professionals, their distinctive but complementary nature was discussed, and the advantages and disadvantages of each adult role for the child concerned was noted. A key task for the future will be to find a way of encouraging closer working relationships between parents and pre-school workers without alienating or demoralising those for whom partnership presents problems. It is important not to create a situation in which parents are no longer able to relax and enjoy their children because of additional responsibilities and tasks they have been urged to take on. Equally, professional workers should not feel their own professionalism or 'expertise' is undervalued or undermined as their job takes on new dimensions and their role begins to change.

On the basis of observations and discussions in the 130 centres, nurseries and schemes the project team visited, partnership was defined as:

> 'a working relationship that is characterised by a shared sense of purpose, mutual respect, and the willingness to negotiate. This implies a sharing of information, responsibility, skills, decision-making and accountability'.

The project identified many different ways in which staff and parents were working towards such a partnership, and many different roles that parents were playing: as supporters, learners, helpers, teachers, carers, group leaders, volunteers, policy makers and managers. There was however considerable confusion in the minds of many of those working in the centres as to what their objectives were in working with parents, and on whose terms the relationship was to be conducted. Was it partnership they were working towards, or simply more support from parents? To help clarify thinking and provide a tool for staff to re-examine their own work, the project team devised the framework of parent involvement given in chapter 7, covering the five main areas of non-participation, support, participation, partnership and control. This was not intended to imply a progression from one dimension to another, but to reflect the range of tasks and relationships currently described as partnership or involvement.

Finally we have looked at those different factors which can help or hinder partnership – what we have called 'partnership proneness'. It was clear from the visits to centres and from the case studies that the aims and purpose of a centre were crucial in determining what kind of relationships would develop – was the centre complementing or compensating for parents' relationships with their own children? Was there a policy on work with parents, and was it clearly stated and understood? How was the centre managed, and were parents involved in management other than in token ways? Was additional funding available? Were parents exploited in their role as workers? How accessible was the centre, and how welcoming? Did parents feel a sense of ownership, or were they always on someone else's territory? And what kinds of methods and strategies did staff adopt to ensure that they reached out to *all* parents, and not just the enthusiastic and confident few? Was there something for parents, as well as for children? Did parents feel they were being listened to and taken seriously? Or were all decisions made when they weren't there?

Working in partnership is a process which takes time to develop. For many parents and professionals it also requires a change in attitude: it is a challenge to their expectations and requires a new look at their roles. It may mean developing new skills, learning to talk and listen in new ways, perhaps taking on different responsibilities. And for professionals in particular it will lead to demands for additional support, training and supervision.

Issues arising from partnership

Measuring the success of partnership

Our primary concern in exploring parent-professional partnership has been in the quality of the relationships between parents and children, between parents and workers and between parents and other parents. A nursery full of parents does not necessarily demonstrate partnership! If *all* parents are to feel equally valued, and are to have access to information and decision-making, then the *process* of consultation and involvement, and the attitudes of the staff will count for more than a programme in which the same three or four parents volunteer for all the jobs that need doing.

On whose terms is this relationship?

There has been an inherent tension running throughout this study. Is parent involvement seen as a means of enabling and empowering parents to become more confident and take on greater responsibilities in relation to their children in particular and the centre and the community in general? Or is it seen as a way of improving the skills and attitudes of parents, and involving them on professionals' terms to help and support the work of the nursery or centre? Where does the power-base lie, and on whose terms is the relationship negotiated? A fundamental stumbling block in many centres visited was the lack of clarity about aims and objectives – why are we here, and what are we trying to do? Without this, it was difficult to work towards a common sense of purposes, and to look at whether the values underlying the work with children and with parents could be shared by all parties.

Involving parents in the educational process

Lack of clarity about the aims and objectives was particularly e
the difficulty that workers in many centres had in articulating
was they were trying to do with children – what in nursery sch
classes might be described as the curriculum. Even when the
worked out a detailed programme, they did not find it easy to
thinking into words and share it with parents. There h
controversy for many years over how much parents should be '
their children before they start in a playgroup or nursery, but as
recent study (1988) has shown, many parents *are* specifically
their young children, and children's reading and maths attai
eight years old was found to be directly related to their lite
numeracy at four. There are thus considerable challenges for w
all pre-school settings in finding ways of sharing with par
understanding of how children learn, and of the role of pa
professionals in supporting that learning.

Parents' needs and choice

The study has demonstrated a blurring of roles between son
and some professionals, and has shown that parents can tak
ranging responsibilities, developing what we have des
reciprocity and 'equivalent expertise'. The importance of star
parents *are* rather than where professionals think they ough
also been stressed, and of the potential for growth in confid
enabling and supportive approach is adopted. Not all parents
will either want to or be able to take on such responsibilities
needs and vulnerabilities should be acknowledged and not de
pursuit of partnership.

Professionals' needs and choice

Most of those working with children under five have been
work with children rather than adults. It is important to rec
not all workers feel able to work in partnership with parents
any case, they will need to develop new skills and be abl
additional training, support and resources. At a time of cut-b
and services in the pre-school field, workers may fear that
providing a cheap alternative to replacing professional staff

* We need to evaluate parent-pr

   to assess the achievements,
   professionals, the children

* Finally, we need to ask whether
services with partnership?

   Child protection and preve
   that some parents canno
   contractual obligations a
   partnership.

This study has looked at the
perspective of the parents and the
the justification for partnership is r
parent and professional working
skills and experience of children,
political or ideological rhetoric and
of children.

References

Aldrich, R. & Leighton P. (1985) *Education: time for a new Act?* Bedford Way Papers 23, London: University Institute of Education

Atkin, J & Bastiani J. (1985) *Preparing Teachers to Work with Parents: a survey of initial training* Nottingham: University School of Education

Aplin, G. & Tristran S. (ed). (1987) *Parents in Partnership,* NCB/SCAFA

Barker, W. (1984) *Child Development Programme* Bristol: Early Child Development Unit, Bristol University

Benn, C. (1981) *Attacking Poverty Through Participation* Pit Publishing, Australia

Bennett, W.S. & Hokenstad, M.C. (1973) 'Full-time people workers and conceptions of the professional' in Halmos P. (ed) *Professionalism and Social Change* Keele University

Blatchford, P. *et al* (1982) *The First Transition: Home to Pre-school* Windsor: NFER/Nelson

Bloom, B.S. (1964) *Stability and Change in Human Characteristics* Wiley, New York

Bronfenbrenner, U. (1974) *Is early intervention effective? A report on longitudinal evaluation of pre-school programmes, vol 2* Washington, Department of Health, Education and Welfare

Chaplais, J. (1986) 'Parents as health record keepers' in De'Ath and Pugh (eds) *Partnership Paper 8* National Children's Bureau

Clement J.R.B. *et al* (1984) *Changed Lives: the effects of the Perry Pre-school Program on youths through age 19* Monograph 8, Ypsilanti, Michigan, High Scope

Committee of Enquiry into the Education of Handicapped Children and Young People (1978) *Special Educational Needs* (Warnock report) HMSO

Committee on Child Health Services (1976) *Fit for the Future* (Court report) HMSO

Cunningham, C. & Davis H. (1985) *'Working with Parents: Frameworks for Collaboration* Open University

Davie, R. (1985) 'Equalities and inequalities in working together for children' in De'Ath and Pugh (eds) *Partnership paper 3* National Children's Bureau

Davis, H. (1985) 'Developing the role of parent advisor in the child health service' in De'Ath and Pugh (eds) *Partnership paper 3* National Children's Bureau

Davis, J. (1985) 'Sharing care in hospital' in De'Ath and Pugh (eds) *Partnership Paper 4* National Children's Bureau

De'Ath, E. (1985) Self Help and Family Centres. A current initiative in helping the community, National Children's Bureau

De'Ath, E. and Pugh G. (eds) (1986) *Working with Parents; a training resource pack* National Children's Bureau

De'Ath, E. and Pugh G. (eds) (1985–6) *Partnership Papers 1–8* National Children's Bureau

1. *Working together; parents and professionals as partners*
2. *Parent involvement; what does it mean and how doe we achieve it?*
3. *Working together with children with special needs; implications for pre-school services*
4. *Sharing the care of children: partnership with parents*
5. *Parents as pre-school workers: examining roles and boundaries*
6. *Partnership with parents: a contract in stress*
7. *Planning and managing pre-school services: is there a role for parents?*
8. *Developing a partnership with parents in the child health services*

Department of Education and Science and Welsh Office (1977) *A New Partnership for our Schools* (Taylor Report) HMSO

Department of Health and Social Security and Welsh Office (1988) *Working together: a guide to arrangements for multi-agency co-operation for the protection of children from abuse* HMSO

Douglas, J.W.B. (1964) *The Home and the School* MacGibbon and Kee

Douglas, J.W.B. *et al.* (1968) *All our Future* Peter Davies

Eisenstadt, N. (1985) 'Sharing management' in De'Ath and Pugh (eds) *Partnership Paper 2* National Children's Bureau

Eyeington J. & Godfrey, M. (1985) 'Towards partnership in a residential family assessment centre' in De'Ath and Pugh *Partnership Paper 6*

Ferri, E. and Niblett, R. (1977) *Disadvantaged Families and Playgroups* NFER/Nelson

Ferri, E. *et al* (1981) *Combined Nursery Centres* Macmillan

Filkin, E. (ed), (1984) *Women and Children First; Home-Link – a neighbourhood education* Michigan; High Scope

Finch, J. (1984) 'The deceit of self-help: pre-school playgroups and working class mothers' *Journal of Social Policy* 13, 1, 1–20

Gilkes, J. (1989) 'Coming to terms with sexual abuse – a day care perspective' *Children and Society* 2, 3

Gilroy, D. (1982) 'Evolving community-based services' in *Social Work Service*, Summer, no. 30

Gordon, I.J. (1969) 'Developing parent power' in Grotberg E (ed) *Critical Issues in Research Related to Disadvantaged Children* Princeton, New Jersey: Educational Testing Service

Greenwood, E. (1966) 'The elements of professionalisation' in Vollmer, H.M. and Mills, D.C. (eds) *Professionalisation* Prentice-Hall

Hadley, R. & McGrath, M. (eds) (1980) *Going Local: neighbourhood social services* NCVO occasional paper 1.

Hall, D., Lowe, R. and Macfarlane A. (eds) (1989) *Health for All Children*, Oxford University Press

Halsey, A.H. (ed) (1972) *Educational Priority: EPA Problems and Policies* Vol 1, HMSO

Hunt, J. McV, (1961) *Intelligence and Experience* New York: Ronald Press

Illich, I, *et al* (1977) *Disabling Professions* Marion Boyars

Johnson, N. (1981) *Voluntary Social Services*, Blackwell and Robertson.

Jones, D. & Mayo, M. (1974) *Community Work; One* Routledge

Jowett, S & Sylva K (1986) 'Does kind of pre-school matter?' *Educational Research* 28, 1

Katz, L. (1982) 'Contemporary perspectives on the roles of mothers and teachers' in *Australian Journal of Early Childhood* 7, 1, 4–15

Laishley, J. (1985) *Parents involvement: developments in pre-schooling and the early school years* National Nursery Examination Board

Laishley, J. & Lindon, L. (1980) 'Schemes of parental involvement in pre-school centres' *Early Childhood* 1, 2, 16–19

Lowe, R. (1986) 'Parents and health visitors: partners in child development' in De'Ath & Pugh (eds) *Partnership Paper 8* NCB

Macbeth, A. (1984) *The child between: a report on school-family relations in the countries of the European Community* Brussels: Commission of the European Community

Mayall, B. (1986) *Keeping Children Healthy* Allen and Unwin

Midwinter, E. (1977) 'The professional-lay relationship: a Victorian legacy' *Journal of Child Psychology and Psychiatry* 18, 101–113

Mittler P. and Mittler H. (1982) *Partnership with Parents* National Council for Special Education

National Children's Bureau (1987) *Investing in the Future: Child health ten years after the Court report.* Report of the Policy and Practice Review Group, National Children's Bureau.

New, C. & David, M. (1985) *For the Children's Sake* Penguin

Newson, J. and Newson E. (1976) *Seven Years Old in the Home Environment* Allen and Unwin

Nicholl, A. (1986) 'New approaches to child health and care: is there a role for parents?' in De'Ath and Pugh (eds) *Partnership Paper 8* National Children's Bureau

Osborn A. *et al* (1984) *The Social Life of Britain's Five Year Olds* Routledge and Kegan Paul

Pre-school Playgroups Association (1987) *The MSC and Under Fives Groups. A survey by the PPA* PPA

Pugh, G. (1988) *Services for Under Fives: developing a coordinated approach* National Children's Bureau

Pugh, G. and De'Ath, E. (1984) *The Needs of Parents: practice and policy in parent education* Macmillan (NCB series)

Pugh, G, Aplin, G, De'Ath, E, and Moxon M (1987a) *Partnership in Action: working with parents in pre-school centres* Volume 1, National Children's Bureau

Pugh G. *et al* (1987b) *Partnership in Action: working with parents in pre-school centres* volume 2, National Children's Bureau

Robinson, J. (1982) *An Evaluation of Health Visiting* Council for the Education and Training of Health Visitors

Scott, G. & Hill, D. (1986) 'Social strategy and under fives' *Community Care* May

Shinman, S. (1981) *A chance for Every Child: access and response to pre-school provision* Tavistock

Smith, T. (1980) *Parents and Pre-school* Grant McIntyre

Tizard, B. *et al* (1981) *Involving Parents in Nursery and Infant Schools* Grant McIntyre

Tizard, B. *et al* (1988) *Young Children at School in the Inner City* Hove: Lawrence Erlbaun Associates

Tizard, B. & Hughes M. (1984) *Young Children Learning* Fonta

Van der Eyken, W. (1982) *Home Start, A four year evaluation* Leicester: Home Start Consultancy

Van der Eyken, W. (1983) *Pre-schooling in Britain* Bristol: Department of Child Health, University of Bristol

Van der Eyken, W. (1984) *Day Nurseries in Action: a national study of local authority day nurseries in England 1975–1983* Bristol: Department of Child Health, University of Bristol

Van der Eyken, W. (1987) *The DHSS Under Fives Initiative 1983–87. Final Report* Bristol: University Institute of Child Health

Watt, J. & Flett, M. (1985) *Continuity in Early Education: the role of parents:* Department of Education, University of Aberdeen

Wolfendale, S. (1983) *Parental Participation in Children's Development and Education* Gordon & Breach

World Health Organisation (1978) *Primary Health Care* WHO/UNICEF

Woodhead, M. (1985) 'Pre-school education has long term effects: but can they be generalised?' *Oxford Review of Education* 11, 2, 133–155